TALK ABOUT TRIVIA
1001 QUESTIONS

Irene E. Schoenberg

Executive Editor: Joanne Dresner
Project Editor: Penny Laporte
Text Design: Laura Ierardi
Cover Design and Illustrations: Kenny Beck
Production: Eduardo Castillo

Talk About Trivia

Longman Inc., 95 Church Street, White Plains, N.Y. 10601

Associated companies: Longman Group Ltd., London; Longman Cheshire Pty.,
Melbourne; Longman Paul Pty., Auckland; Copp Clark Pitman, Toronto;
Pitman Publishing Inc., Boston

Library of Congress Cataloging in Publication Data

Schoenberg, Irene, 1946–
  Talk about trivia.

  1. English language—Text-books for foreign speakers.
2. Questions and answers. I. Title.
PE1128.S3457 1986   428.3′4   85-23820
ISBN 0-582-90721-7

        88 89 9 8 7 6 5 4 3

Distributed in the United Kingdom by Longman Group Ltd., Longman House, Burnt Mill,
Harlow, Essex CM20 2JE, England, and by associated companies, branches and
representatives throughout the world.

Printed in the U.S.A.

For Rita and Paul Steiner
and
Jacques and Estelle Schoenberg

Acknowledgments

I would like to thank all my friends and colleagues who let me **chew their ears off** (#1002) while talking about trivia.

A very special thanks to Pamela McPartland, Director of the International English Language Institute at Hunter College for her invaluable support, enthusiasm and suggestions; to Mary Jerome, Chairperson of the American Language Program of Columbia University for her encouragement throughout this project; and to Ellen Lehrburger of the American Language Program of Columbia University for her support, helpful comments and constructive criticism.

I am indebted to my colleagues at the International English Language Institute and the American Language Program for field testing the questions and offering many valuable suggestions. In particular I would like to mention Winifred Falcon, Karen Brockman and Linda Ferreira. Carlos Yorio, Director of the ESL Department at Lehman College, CUNY, was wonderful about field testing the questions in his Tutorial Program and offering fine recommendations.

A big thanks to all my students at the International English Language Institute and the American Language Program who played the game and laughed and learned and encouraged me to want to write more.

My reviewers Karen Davy, Mona Scheraga, Elizabeth Tannenbaum and Martha Terilli certainly added to the book.

I want to thank my editors Joanne Dresner and Penny Laporte for their fine judgment and discriminating taste. It was wonderful working with them.

My family were unwavering in their support and love throughout. To Harris, Dani, Dahlia, Rita, Paul and Jacques, an extra thanks from the bottom of my heart.

Contents

Introduction

I. The purpose of **Talk About Trivia**

From the quiz shows of the 1950s to the trivia games of the eighties, millions of people have been thrilled by the experience of matching wits with others. Students of English as a Second Language are no exception. Taking advantage of this phenomenon, **Talk About Trivia: 1001 Questions** challenges the skills of high beginning and intermediate level students—or even young native born Americans—as it helps them to learn aspects of American language and culture in an enjoyable way. Through a series of questions and answers either played as a game or used as a springboard for conversation, vocabulary or grammar classes, students become familiar with important features of American language and civilization.

The questions grew out of years of classroom experience. Many were student inspired. Some questions were included to help foreign students avoid embarrassing situations in the United States. The question about sympathy cards, for example, was included in response to the flow of sympathy cards sent by ESL students at the end of the term to "sympatico" ESL teachers. Other questions consider students' practical needs such as asking for the rest room or ordering in a restaurant. Most of all, the questions were written for students to have fun while improving their knowledge of American language and lore.

II. Components

Talk About Trivia: 1001 Questions includes six discrete categories. Three provide information about American civilization and culture: **General Knowledge about the United States**, **American Holidays and Special Occasions**, and **American History, Geography and Government**. And three focus on language: **Phrases and Idioms**, **Vocabulary**, and **Grammar**.

The book is further divided into Part One, intended for high beginning or low intermediate students, and Part Two, for intermediate students. In general Part One is easier in both language and information called for than Part Two. However, to give the game an element of chance, there are a few more difficult questions in Part One and a few easier questions in Part Two. The perforated answer key at the back of the book permits use of the text for self-study as well as in a classroom setting.

III. Uses of **Talk About Trivia**

Talk About Trivia is not a basic text but it adds to basic texts in a variety of ways. It offers a cultural component that can be quantified. It gives the teacher hundreds of items that stimulate interesting conversations. It allows false beginners to shine in cultural areas while it triggers their interest in vocabulary, grammar, and two-word verbs. The book can be used in game format, in discussion, vocabulary or grammar classes, and in tutorial programs. It is easy and fun to use in self-study.

A. For Classroom Use as a Game

The book works equally well in large classes, small ones or in competition between two classes. Students and teachers have enjoyed using the following three stage method for playing the game in class.

Stage 1 *Preparation.*   Separate the book into sixteen units, each unit containing one page of questions from each category. Using six different categories allows students to recognize their areas of strength and weakness.

Divide the class into small groups. Group members work together answering all the questions in the unit selected for that session. A great deal of incidental learning takes place as students work hard helping teammates who may not understand a question. The teacher goes from group to group answering questions and checking to make sure all the answers are correct. After all groups have completed the unit, the class is ready for the review.

Stage 2 *Review.*   The teacher or students ask questions from the unit just studied and add questions from past units. The class calls out the correct answer. After a rapid review of about five minutes, students are ready to play the game.

Stage 3 *The Game.*   The teams set up in Stage 1 remain for the game. To begin, the teacher or a student acting as a Master of Ceremonies for the game, places category labels (from page 115) in a hat and a student from the first team picks a category. This student becomes the spokesperson for the team, but everyone on the team helps choose the correct answer. The teacher or Master of Ceremonies asks a question from the category selected. If the second team thinks the answer is incorrect, it can challenge the answer. If the second team gets it wrong, the next team can try. The team that gets the correct answer wins a point. After the first person on the first team has a turn, the first person on the next team picks a category. This continues until everyone on each team has had at least one turn. Each correct answer gives the team one point. The team with the most points wins.

Variations.

1. Each student asks one question to each team, including his own. The object is to ask one's team an easy question and one's opponents' teams difficult questions.

2. Eliminate the multiple choices in all but the grammar section of the book to make the game more challenging.

3. Have a time limit of thirty seconds to answer each question.

4. Double the Score. Students choose a new question from a unit they have not yet studied for double points.

5. Put on a quiz show. One student acts as a Master of Ceremonies, interviews contestants, gives away magnificent prizes or billions of dollars while playing his version of **Talk About Trivia**.

6. Play the board game on the back page. The game requires one die, pieces which move around the board and an unmarked book of **Talk About Trivia: 1001 Questions**. The first person or team to get a correct answer in every category wins.

B. For Discussion

1. Select a page from the **General Knowledge about the United States** or **American Holidays and Special Occasions** section. Have groups of students find out how each question on the page relates to the countries and backgrounds of those in the group. A spokesperson reports back to the class.

2. Select a few questions from the **General Knowledge about the United States** or **American Holidays and Special Occasions** section that relate to one subject (for example superstitions, food, sports, weddings, new years). Ask students to form groups to discuss how those customs relate to their country. The focus on content encourages spontaneous and meaningful language practice.

3. Questions about the geography, the flag, the national anthem, or the presidents of the United States act as springboards for discussion about other countries.

4. Use of the collage preceding each section helps students become interested in and familiar with questions from that category.

C. For Grammar Classes

The **Grammar** section focuses on problem areas for beginning students. Each question can serve as a review or an introduction to a point of grammar. Other sections can give students practice in using grammatical patterns in context, teaching them indirectly. For example:

a) *Superlatives* are recurrent in the *geography* questions;

b) The *simple present tense* is used in most of the *general knowledge* and *holiday* questions;

c) *Mass/count nouns* are practiced in the *vocabulary*, and *phrases* and *idioms* questions. "I'd like to make a toast" versus "I'd like to make some toast" highlights the importance of learning the count/non-count distinction;

d) *Present time clauses* are salient *throughout* the book;

e) The *definite article* occurs in the *geography* questions;

f) The *simple past tense* is prominent in the *history* questions.

D. For Vocabulary Classes

Many of the distractors in the vocabulary, and phrases and idioms questions come from classroom experience. Once when a student wanted to know the word for a man getting married, a classmate called out "the broom." He was quickly corrected by another student who smiled and said, "Not the broom, the gloom." Another time, a student talked about eating a "kitchen in the chicken," with a cup of hot "soap."

Playing the game over again helps students become so familiar and comfortable with the words that they become a part of their active vocabulary. Teachers may use the vocabulary selections for word games and the idioms and phrases for role play.

After studying the vocabulary section, groups of students in higher levels may enjoy working together and writing their own vocabulary questions, using the distractors as the words to be defined.

E. For Student-Created Games

Using the questions about American culture and civilization as a model, groups of students or individual students create their own trivia game asking questions about their countries. They then produce a quiz show in which other students become the contestants.

F. For Tutorials

Teacher aids or volunteers using the text in small informal groups find communication flows naturally from the desire to share and compare cultures and ideas.

G. For Self-Study

By simply going over the questions and answers several times, a student can absorb a great deal of knowledge. (Students should avoid writing in their text so that they can retest themselves).

Consider the above instructions as guidelines or suggestions that need not limit the application of these materials. I'm certain that teachers and students will create their own novel ways of using the questions. My main hope is that students will enjoy learning English as they **Talk About Trivia**.

General Knowledge about the United States

PART ONE

Very interesting person...very important

Directions: Complete the sentences.

1. People usually **tip** _____.
   a) movie ushers
   b) taxi drivers
   c) teachers

2. **Brunch** is a combination of breakfast and lunch. Americans usually eat brunch on _____.
   a) Sunday
   b) Tuesday
   c) Friday

3. At the movies people often eat _____.
   a) **popcorn**
   b) **grapes**
   c) **nuts**

4. In restaurants we usually leave a _____.
   a) **25–35% tip**
   b) **10–20% tip**
   c) **40–50% tip**

5. A **professor** teaches in a _____.
   a) high school
   b) junior high school
   c) college or university

6. **English muffins**, **french toast** and **danish pastry** are _____.
   a) Rock groups from Europe
   b) popular foods
   c) dances from Europe

7. Many people think the number **thirteen** brings _____.
   a) happiness
   b) money
   c) bad luck

8. A **VIP** is a _____.
   a) very important person
   b) very interesting person
   c) very intelligent person

9. **NBC, CBS** and **ABC** are _____.
   a) government agencies
   b) medical groups
   c) television stations

10. **Kindergartens** are for _____.
    a) five-year-olds
    b) teen-agers
    c) flowers

11. **12 P.M.** is _____.
    a) lunch time
    b) bed time
    c) dinner time

12. The paper money in the United States is _____.
    a) **the dollar**
    b) **the pound**
    c) **the penny**

13. Most **movies** are made in _____.
    a) San Francisco
    b) Chicago
    c) Hollywood

14. A **spelling bee** is _____.
    a) a flying insect
    b) a spelling contest
    c) a speeding car

15. **Albert Einstein** was an American _____.
    a) poet
    b) scientist
    c) artist

16. When a teacher enters the class, the students _____.
    a) **stand up**
    b) **clap**
    c) **look up**

17. The **check room** in a restaurant is the place to _____.
    a) pay for your meal
    b) leave your coat
    c) wash your hands

18. Four **common last names** in the United States are _____.
    a) Jack, Mary, Daniel, Janet
    b) Johnson, Smith, Brown, Jones
    c) Billy, Jimmy, Suzy, Scottie

19. At **7 P.M.** and **11 P.M.** many people watch _____.
    a) quiz shows
    b) cartoons
    c) the news

20. There are no **TV advertisements** for _____.
    a) cigarettes
    b) toys
    c) shampoo

21. **Elvis Presley** was the king of _____.
    a) Country Western music
    b) Jazz
    c) Rock and Roll

22. The **shortest day** of the year is _____.
    a) June 21
    b) December 21
    c) March 21

23. *Newsweek* and *Time* are the names of _____.
    a) newspapers
    b) TV programs
    c) magazines

24. A movie **rated "G"** means the movie is OK for _____.
    a) girls
    b) grown-ups
    c) everyone

25. **Muhammed Ali** is a boxer. His name used to be _____.
    a) Mr. T.
    b) Omar Khayyam
    c) Cassius Clay

26. A car with the letters **MD** on the license plate belongs to a _____.
    a) diplomat
    b) doctor
    c) detective

27. **Snoopy** is a famous comic strip _____.
    a) dog
    b) detective
    c) pilot

28. **Dustin Hoffman, Paul Newman** and **Robert Redford** are famous _____.
    a) journalists
    b) baseball players
    c) actors

29. Many stores close every _____.
    a) **afternoon**
    b) **Sunday**
    c) **Saturday**

30. A popular show for very young children is called _____.
    a) **Sesame Street**
    b) **Sesame Seed**
    c) **Open Sesame**

31. Americans often eat **raw** _____.
    a) fish
    b) meat
    c) vegetables

32. **Lucille Ball, Woody Allen, Bill Cosby** and **Jerry Lewis** are _____.
    a) singers
    b) dancers
    c) comedians

33. When you **set the table**, you put the knife and spoon _____.
    a) to the right of the plate
    b) to the left of the plate
    c) above the plate

34. You put your **thumb up**. That means someone _____.
    a) did very badly
    b) did very well
    c) sneezed

35. Children **attend public school** from _____.
    a) September through June
    b) October through July
    c) November through August

36. In business, when people reach an agreement, they usually _____.
    a) **bow**
    b) **shake hands**
    c) **wave**

37. A student wants **to ask a question** in class. He should raise _____.
    a) two fingers
    b) his eyebrows
    c) his hand

38. In the United States you can write the date **January 4, 1946**, _____.
    a) 1/4/46
    b) 4/1/46
    c) 46/4/1

39. **Young married couples** usually live in _____.
    a) the home of the wife's parents
    b) the home of the husband's parents
    c) their own home

40. Some people think it is **bad luck** to break _____.
    a) a window
    b) a mirror
    c) a glass

41. The **dollar sign** is _____.
    a) $
    b) ¢
    c) D

42. Americans usually wear their **wedding rings** _____.
    a) on the fourth finger of the right hand
    b) on the fourth finger of the left hand
    c) on the fifth finger of either hand

43. **Eleven o'clock in the morning** in New York is _____.
    a) eight o'clock in the morning in California
    b) two o'clock in the afternoon in California
    c) eleven o'clock in the morning in California

44. Most people eat their **biggest meal** _____.
    a) in the morning
    b) at noon
    c) in the evening

45. For **lunch** many children eat _____.
    a) bread and chocolate
    b) meat pies and pudding
    c) peanut butter and jelly sandwiches

46. The **NBA** is _____.
    a) the National Birdwatchers Association
    b) the National Boaters Association
    c) the National Basketball Association

47. The **average work week** is _____.
    a) 45-50 hours
    b) 25-30 hours
    c) 35-40 hours

48. When you go to a friend's house, you **take off** your _____.
    a) shoes
    b) coat
    c) jewelry

49. For **breakfast** people often eat _____.
    a) eggs
    b) soup
    c) salad

50. A woman who is **six feet tall** is _____.
    a) very short
    b) very tall
    c) medium height

51. If you find a **four leaf clover**, you will _____.
    a) fall in love
    b) fall off a ladder
    c) have good luck

52. People often **kiss** _____.
    a) when they are first introduced
    b) when they see a close friend after a long time
    c) whenever they see a friend

53. The second most widely spoken language in the United States
    is _____.
    a) **Spanish**
    b) **Italian**
    c) **Chinese**

54. When you write to your uncle Daniel and his wife, Gabrielle, you write
    to _____.
    a) **Mr. and Mrs. Daniel Evans**
    b) **Mr. and Mrs. Gabrielle Evans**
    c) **Mrs. and Mr. Daniel Evans**

55. Your teacher's name is Victor Barnes. You **call him** _____.
    a) Barnes
    b) teacher
    c) Mr. Barnes

56. **Ms.** is the title used before the last name of _____.
    a) only married women
    b) only unmarried women
    c) married and unmarried women

57. You buy tickets for a play at the _____.
    a) **post office**
    b) **box office**
    c) **Oval Office**

58. **Jesse Owens** won a gold medal at the 1936 Olympics for _____.
    a) running
    b) swimming
    c) basketball

59. What sports event takes place **in a diamond**? _____
    a) hockey
    b) baseball
    c) volleyball

60. **During a meal**, people in the United States _____.
    a) never talk
    b) rarely talk
    c) usually talk

61. A person **bows** when he has _____.
    a) met a friend
    b) sung or danced for many people
    c) met an older person

62. The **most popular pet** in the United States is the _____.
    a) chicken
    b) rabbit
    c) dog

63. You need help with a telephone call so you ask for the _____.
    a) **call girl**
    b) **operator**
    c) **police**

64. The **weekend** is _____.
    a) Saturday and Sunday
    b) Sunday
    c) Saturday

65. You are talking about a dog. You can only use the pronoun _____.
    a) **he**
    b) **he** or **it**
    c) **he, she** or **it**

66. **Popeye the Sailorman** became strong by eating _____.
    a) yogurt
    b) spinach
    c) seaweed

67. Most **factory jobs** are _____.
    a) five days a week
    b) four and a half days a week
    c) five and a half days a week

68. The **work day** usually **ends** at _____.
    a) three-thirty in the afternoon
    b) four-thirty in the afternoon
    c) five o'clock in the evening

69. Mickey Mouse, Donald Duck and Goofy were created by _____.
    a) **Mary Poppins**
    b) **Mother Goose**
    c) **Walt Disney**

70. **People** usually **eat dinner** _____.
    a) between six and eight in the evening
    b) between eight and ten in the evening
    c) between three and five in the afternoon

71. Most **Americans over 65** years old want to live in _____.
    a) old homes
    b) their own homes
    c) their children's homes

72. The **average American lives** about _____.
    a) 65 years
    b) 70 years
    c) 75 years

73. Your **zip code** is a part of your _____.
    a) pants
    b) name
    c) address

74. In the 1920s, the **Charleston** was a popular _____.
    a) dance
    b) song
    c) restaurant

75. Radios have **AM** and _____.
    a) **PM** frequencies
    b) **FM** frequencies
    c) **GM** frequencies

76. A typical **American dessert** is _____.
    a) apple pie
    b) sweetbreads
    c) pancakes

77. You can buy notebooks and pens at a _____.
    a) **post office**
    b) **record store**
    c) **stationery store**

78. You can **bargain** in most stores _____.
    a) all of the time
    b) most of the time
    c) none of the time

79. **Harry Houdini** was a famous _____.
    a) magician
    b) composer
    c) politician

80. Most people take a **coffee break** between _____.
    a) twelve and one o'clock
    b) ten and eleven o'clock
    c) eight and nine o'clock

81. **Dr. Martin Luther King, Jr.** won the Nobel Prize for _____.
    a) medicine
    b) literature
    c) peace

82. At a **cafeteria** people _____.
    a) serve themselves
    b) eat only fast foods
    c) leave a tip

83. The **longest day of the year** comes at the beginning of _____.
    a) spring
    b) summer
    c) winter

84. A **touchdown** is good in _____.
    a) dancing
    b) football
    c) running

Phrases and Idioms
PART ONE

Directions: Complete the sentences.

85. I need a tissue. My **nose is** _____.
    a) **walking**
    b) **running**
    c) **jumping**

86. Someone **pulling your leg** is _____.
    a) selling you shoes
    b) helping you grow
    c) joking with you

87. Your car is **out of gas**. It _____.
    a) doesn't have any gas
    b) has a lot of gas
    c) has a little gas

10

88. Something **costs an arm and a leg**. It is _____.
    a) free
    b) expensive
    c) cheap

89. Young children don't like to wait. They want everything _____.
    a) **right away**
    b) **right over**
    c) **right on**

90. Something **out of this world** is _____.
    a) fantastic
    b) terrible
    c) useless

91. When you are **window shopping**, you are _____.
    a) shopping for windows
    b) buying kitchen curtains
    c) looking at store windows

92. Someone says, "**I'll give you a ring**." You expect him to _____.
    a) marry you
    b) walk around you
    c) telephone you

93. If a person **works like a dog**, he _____.
    a) is very friendly
    b) listens very carefully
    c) works very hard

94. When you lower the sound of a stereo, you _____.
    a) **pull it down**
    b) **turn it down**
    c) **put it down**

95. A **senior citizen** is _____.
    a) an important person
    b) a person over sixty-five
    c) a United States senator

96. You learn a language _____.
    a) **step-by-step**
    b) **line-by-line**
    c) **inch-by-inch**

97. A man with **a good head on his shoulders** is _____.
    a) handsome
    b) strong
    c) intelligent

98. **Handmade clothes** are _____.
    a) clothes that you wear on your hand
    b) clothes that someone sewed by hand
    c) bracelets, rings and watches

99. A **traffic jam** is _____.
    a) something sweet that goes on bread
    b) many cars trying to move in one area
    c) an automobile accident

100. When you eat in a restaurant, you _____.
    a) **eat out**
    b) **eat in**
    c) **eat up**

101. You want to relax for a short time during work. You _____.
    a) **take a chance**
    b) **take a nap**
    c) **take a break**

102. Linda is an **only child**. She doesn't have _____.
    a) friends or neighbors
    b) a mother or father
    c) sisters or brothers

103. **Take off** your sweater! It's _____.
    a) hot
    b) cold
    c) blue

104. The birthday child made a wish and _____.
    a) **blew on** the candles
    b) **blew out** the candles
    c) **blew away** the candles

105. The robber said, "_____."
    a) **Hands up** or I'll shoot
    b) **Hands down** or I'll shoot
    c) **Hands in** or I'll shoot

106. George wants to listen to the radio. Please _____.
    a) **turn it on**
    b) **try it on**
    c) **take it on**

107. **Take it easy** means _____.
    a) repeat
    b) respond
    c) relax

108. The child is _____.
    a) **afraid for** the dark
    b) **afraid of** the dark
    c) **afraid about** the dark

109. Last night I _____.
    a) **dreamed with** you
    b) **dreamed about** you
    c) **dreamed for** you

110. At a gas station you often say, "_____."
    a) **Fill it up**
    b) **Put it on**
    c) **Pour it on**

111. An **out-of-order** sign means a machine _____.
    a) doesn't work
    b) isn't clean
    c) isn't full

112. The clouds are dark. It _____.
    a) **looks as** it's going to rain
    b) **looks up** it's going to rain
    c) **looks like** it's going to rain

113. Jonathan Rogers lost his job. He's _____.
    a) **looking for** a new one
    b) **looking like** a new one
    c) **looking on** a new one

114. Bella likes that red hat. She's _____.
    a) **trying it up**
    b) **trying it out**
    c) **trying it on**

115. Now he can read the newspaper. He has just _____.
    a) **put out** his glasses
    b) **put on** his glasses
    c) **put in** his glasses

116. The cat _____.
    a) **ran after** the rat
    b) **ran out of** the rat
    c) **ran up** the rat

117. You're not watching that program. Please _____.
    a) **turn up** the TV
    b) **turn off** the TV
    c) **turn over** the TV

118. Your coat is on the floor. Your mother told you to _____.
    a) **hang it up**
    b) **hang it on**
    c) **hang it over**

119. He made a lot of mistakes on his report. He had to _____.
    a) **do it in**
    b) **do it under**
    c) **do it over**

120. You are **leaving for** Paris. That means you are _____.
    a) going to Paris
    b) leaving Paris
    c) living in Paris

121. A person in **show business** _____.
    a) paints
    b) designs
    c) entertains

122. You did an excellent job. _____!
    a) **Keep up** the good work
    b) **Keep to** the good work
    c) **Keep on** the good work

123. Her **line is busy**. She _____.
    a) has caught a fish
    b) is talking on the telephone
    c) is drying clothes

124. You **ran into** an old boyfriend. You _____.
    a) met him by surprise
    b) hurt him in an accident
    c) argued with him

125. People who agree _____.
    a) **walk hand-in-hand**
    b) **dance cheek-to-cheek**
    c) **see eye-to-eye**

126. A person with **a green thumb** is a _____.
    a) sick person
    b) bad painter
    c) good gardener

127. You're talking to someone on the telephone when the doorbell rings.
    You ask the person on the phone to _____.
    a) **hold up**
    b) **hold on**
    c) **hold out**

128. A **help wanted** sign means _____.
    a) a job is available
    b) someone is in trouble
    c) a person needs money

129. A **day off** is a day you _____.
    a) feel bad
    b) don't work
    c) don't eat

130. You need a match for your cigarette. You ask, "_____?"
    a) **Do you have a light**
    b) **Do you have the light**
    c) **Do you have light**

131. A woman is **going out with** a man. She is _____.
    a) dating him
    b) leaving him
    c) working for him

132. A person with a **broken heart** needs _____.
    a) an operation
    b) a new heart
    c) a lot of love

133. **Watch your step** means _____.
    a) be careful
    b) don't look up
    c) dance slowly

134. Something **second hand** _____.
    a) is for left-handed people
    b) has already been used
    c) is heavy to lift

135. Today Nancy slept late. She usually _____.
    a) **gets on** early
    b) **gets up** early
    c) **gets down** early

136. When you don't hear someone, you say, "_____"
    a) **Encore! Encore!**
    b) **Excuse me?**
    c) **Repeat yourself.**

137. A person leaves and says, "**Take care.**" He means _____.
    a) get help
    b) take chances
    c) stay well

138. Your friend is at your door. You say, "Please, _____."
    a) **make an entrance**
    b) **come in**
    c) **come over**

139. When you get to class, you **hand** your homework _____.
    a) **in**
    b) **off**
    c) **away**

140. When a person sneezes, you should say, "_____!"
    a) **Stop it**
    b) **To your health**
    c) **God bless you**

141. You want someone to pay attention to you. You should say, "_____."
    a) **Hey you**
    b) **Excuse me**
    c) **Listen here**

142. You may call a waiter, "_____."
    a) **Waiter**
    b) **Boy**
    c) **Man**

143. You want to meet a friend. You might say, "Let's _____."
    a) **sit together**
    b) **get together**
    c) **stay together**

144. A friend returns after being away. You might say, "_____."
    a) **Welcome back**
    b) **You're welcome**
    c) **See you later**

145. At a restaurant who asks, "**Ready to order**?" The _____.
    a) waiter
    b) cashier
    c) customer

146. You meet a friend at 9:00 P.M. You might say, "_____."
    a) **Good night**
    b) **Good-bye**
    c) **Hi**

147. Someone stepped on your toe and said, "Sorry."
    You respond, "_____."
    a) **That's all right**
    b) **All right**
    c) **That's too bad**

148. The person **ahead of you** is _____.
   a) behind you
   b) in front of you
   c) next to you

149. I'll **give you a hand** means I'll _____.
   a) hit you
   b) hug you
   c) help you

150. You can't understand a problem. You try to _____.
   a) **figure it out**
   b) **find it out**
   c) **fill it out**

151. When you telephone your friend Jane, you might say, "Hello. _____"
   a) **Where's Jane**?
   b) **Is Jane there**?
   c) **Bring Jane to the phone**.

152. You are introduced to a new boss. You say, "_____."
   a) **Pleased to meet you**
   b) **Great meeting you**
   c) **Hi there**

153. Someone said you don't understand English. You want to tell the person he's wrong. You say, "_____."
   a) **I'm understanding in English**
   b) **I *do* understand English**
   c) **English is understood by me**

154. People say, "**See you!**" when _____.
   a) entering a class
   b) leaving a room
   c) putting on glasses

155. A friend asks, "**What's up**?" He wants to know about _____.
   a) the stars
   b) the weather
   c) your life

156. My car has a lot of problems. It's a _____.
   a) **banana**
   b) **lemon**
   c) **peach**

157. You don't know where the bathroom is at a friend's house. You ask, "Where is _____?"
   a) **the rest room**
   b) **the bathroom**
   c) **the washing room**

158. When you borrow a book, you should _____.
    a) **give it away**
    b) **give it out**
    c) **give it back**

159. A **soft drink** is a drink _____.
    a) with whipped cream
    b) without ice
    c) without alcohol

160. A person who **feels blue** is _____.
    a) sad
    b) angry
    c) cold

161. She's **all ears** means she _____.
    a) is listening carefully
    b) has big ears
    c) likes music

162. Ralph got sick so the chairperson **called** the meeting _____.
    a) **up**
    b) **off**
    c) **in**

163. An American rooster says, "_____."
    a) **Oink-Oink**
    b) **Yankee-doodle**
    c) **Cock-a-doodle-do**

164. People who like **hot food** like food that is _____.
    a) very warm
    b) very spicy
    c) very sweet

165. When a person says, "Thank you," the correct response is "_____."
    a) **You too**
    b) **Please**
    c) **You're welcome**

166. Luis used to live in his brother's home, but recently he _____.
    a) **moved out**
    b) **moved in**
    c) **moved off**

167. There are a lot of cockroaches in the kitchen. How can we _____?
    a) **get out of them**
    b) **get into them**
    c) **get rid of them**

American Holidays and Special Occasions

PART ONE

Directions: Complete the sentences.

168. What do children wear on **Halloween**? _____.
     a) costumes
     b) pumpkins
     c) new clothes

169. At the first **Thanksgiving** dinner, the Pilgrims ate with _____.
     a) American cowboys
     b) American Indians
     c) the King of England

170. On **Easter** children _____.
     a) throw eggs
     b) eat eggs
     c) decorate eggs

171. **Santa Claus** enters a house through the _____.
     a) chimney
     b) window
     c) back door

172. **In June** there is a holiday for remembering _____.
     a) lovers
     b) nurses
     c) fathers

173. What holiday do turkeys hate? _____.
     a) **Halloween**
     b) **Labor Day**
     c) **Thanksgiving Day**

174. **Thanksgiving** always comes on the fourth _____.
     a) Thursday in November
     b) Tuesday in November
     c) Thursday in October

175. On **New Year's Day** many people in the United States watch _____.
     a) soccer games
     b) football games
     c) baseball games

176. **Flower girls** are often part of _____.
     a) weddings
     b) parades
     c) student protests

177. On **Easter** people frequently wear _____.
     a) new clothes
     b) old clothes
     c) costumes

178. A **sweet sixteen** is a party for _____.
     a) a boy
     b) a girl
     c) a candy lover

179. After **a couple marries**, friends throw _____.
     a) rice on them
     b) water on them
     c) grass on them

180. When **a baby is born**, fathers give out _____.
     a) candy
     b) cigars
     c) cigarettes

181. The only time many American **women wear veils** is on _____.
    a) Valentine's Day
    b) Mother's Day
    c) their wedding day

182. People wear a **cap and gown** on _____.
    a) their wedding day
    b) their graduation day
    c) New Year's Day

183. Men and women wear **party hats** on _____.
    a) Valentine's Day
    b) July 4
    c) New Year's Eve

184. At **a traditional wedding**, you often hear the song, "_____."
    a) She'll Be Coming Around the Mountain
    b) For He's a Jolly Good Fellow
    c) Here Comes the Bride

185. **In early December** young children often send letters to the _____.
    a) North Pole
    b) United Nations
    c) White House

186. **Presents** are usually exchanged on _____.
    a) Columbus Day
    b) Christmas
    c) Lincoln's Birthday

187. When **someone dies,** her friends and relatives often _____.
    a) put a notice in the newspaper
    b) put a sign on their door
    c) wear a black flower on their clothes

188. **February 14** is for _____.
    a) workers
    b) lovers
    c) jokers

189. The **best man** at a wedding is _____.
    a) the father of the bride
    b) the man getting married
    c) the best friend of the groom

190. **Organ music** is very common at _____.
    a) football games
    b) graduation dances
    c) wedding ceremonies

191. When **people marry**, they often ask friends to be _____.
    a) waiters at their wedding
    b) ushers at their wedding
    c) doormen at their wedding

192. People send the most cards at Christmas. The second largest number of cards is sent for _____.
    a) **Thanksgiving**
    b) **July 4**
    c) **Valentine's Day**

193. **Red and green** are _____.
    a) Christmas colors
    b) St. Patrick's Day colors
    c) July 4 colors

194. People blow horns and kiss at midnight on _____.
    a) **July 4**
    b) **New Year's Eve**
    c) **Christmas Eve**

195. **April 1** is also called _____.
    a) April Flower Day
    b) April Shower Day
    c) April Fool's Day

196. Stores are busiest just before _____.
    a) **Labor Day**
    b) **New Year's Day**
    c) **Christmas Day**

197. The **Halloween colors** are _____.
    a) orange and black
    b) orange and green
    c) red, white and blue

198. Bakeries sell cakes for every occasion. On what holiday can you buy a red, white and blue cake? _____.
    a) **Labor Day**
    b) **July 4**
    c) **Lincoln's Birthday**

199. On what holiday do many people in the United States eat pumpkin pie? _____.
    a) **Labor Day**
    b) **Thanksgiving**
    c) **Washington's Birthday**

200. For most students the last holiday before the new school year begins is _____.
    a) **Memorial Day**
    b) **Labor Day**
    c) **Independence Day**

201. There is **no special holiday** in the United States for _____.
    a) soldiers
    b) mothers
    c) teachers

202. "**Auld Lang Syne**" is often sung on _____.
    a) July 4
    b) New Year's Eve
    c) Veteran's Day

203. **Halloween** comes on the last day of _____.
    a) October
    b) September
    c) November

204. A **50th anniversary** is a _____.
    a) silver anniversary
    b) golden anniversary
    c) diamond anniversary

205. On **New Year's Eve** many Americans drink _____.
    a) lemonade
    b) Coca-Cola
    c) champagne

206. **July 4** is _____.
    a) Labor Day
    b) Children's Day
    c) Independence Day

207. **Christmas** always comes on _____.
    a) December 25
    b) December 1
    c) December 31

208. **Valentine's Day** is a day to _____.
    a) give pennies to children
    b) play jokes on friends
    c) give chocolates to sweethearts

209. **Labor Day** comes toward the end of which season? _____.
    a) summer
    b) winter
    c) spring

210. **Easter** comes _____.
    a) in the winter
    b) in the spring
    c) in the summer

211. June 14 is **Flag Day**. The American flag is _____.
    a) red, white and green
    b) blue, white and orange
    c) red, white and blue

212. Who wears a red suit, has a long, white beard and comes from the North Pole? _____.
    a) **The Cookie Monster**
    b) **Mickey Mouse**
    c) **Santa Claus**

213. Which holiday is mostly for children? _____.
    a) **Labor Day**
    b) **Halloween**
    c) **Veteran's Day**

214. A special **Christmas** and **New Year's Day drink** is _____.
    a) hot cider
    b) eggnog
    c) coffee with whipped cream

215. People **vote** on the first Tuesday after the first Monday in _____.
    a) July
    b) October
    c) November

216. People send **Season's Greetings** cards _____.
    a) during the Christmas season
    b) at the beginning of spring
    c) at the beginning of each season

217. Your **fiance** is the man _____.
    a) you are going to marry
    b) you have just married
    c) your daughter has married

218. At Christmas time people sing about **Rudolf**, the red-nosed _____.
    a) rabbit
    b) raccoon
    c) reindeer

219. On **Veteran's Day** we remember _____.
    a) soldiers
    b) animal doctors
    c) presidents

220. What holiday comes on the last Monday in May? _____.
    a) **Mother's Day**
    b) **Memorial Day**
    c) **Flag Day**

221. People go to sleep very late on _____.
    a) **Thanksgiving**
    b) **Valentine's Day**
    c) **New Year's Eve**

222. **In February** we celebrate the birthdays of Abraham Lincoln and _____.
    a) Martin Luther King, Jr.
    b) John F. Kennedy
    c) George Washington

223. There is a famous Christmas song, "I'm dreaming of a _____."
    a) **bright Christmas**
    b) **white Christmas**
    c) **green Christmas**

224. Every four years there is **an extra day** in _____.
    a) December
    b) February
    c) January

225. At **a birthday party** for an eight-year-old, the cake has _____.
    a) seven candles
    b) eight candles
    c) nine candles

226. When do **children look for money** under their pillow? _____
    a) The day after their first haircut
    b) The day after they lose a tooth
    c) The day they begin the first grade

227. On their **wedding day** brides usually don't _____.
    a) dance with their fathers
    b) eat or drink the wedding food
    c) wear black dresses

228. A **honeymoon** is a trip you take _____.
    a) by yourself
    b) to the moon
    c) with your new husband or wife

229. We say, "**Close your eyes and make a wish**" before you _____.
    a) go out on Halloween
    b) blow out your birthday candles
    c) get married

230. **At a wedding** you wear _____.
    a) your birthday suit
    b) jeans and a T-shirt
    c) a suit or dress

231. You usually don't buy **a baby boy** _____.
    a) pink clothes
    b) red clothes
    c) blue clothes

232. You say "**Happy Anniversary**" when _____.
    a) a person is celebrating the day she was born
    b) a couple is celebrating the day they got married
    c) a person is celebrating her graduation from school

233. **Hearts** are the symbol of _____.
    a) Mother's Day
    b) Veteran's Day
    c) Valentine's Day

234. At a wedding, the woman getting married is called the **bride**. The man is called the _____.
    a) **broom**
    b) **gloom**
    c) **groom**

235. The **birthday of the United States** is on _____.
    a) January 1
    b) July 4
    c) March 21

236. Friends may decorate your car on your _____.
    a) **30th birthday**
    b) **graduation day**
    c) **wedding day**

237. An **important birthday** is a _____.
    a) 17th birthday
    b) 29th birthday
    c) 21st birthday

238. At **children's birthday parties**, children often play "Pin the Tail on the _____."
    a) Pig
    b) Whale
    c) Donkey

239. Children invite friends to sleep at their house for _____.
    a) **pajama** parties
    b) **dream** parties
    c) **star** parties

240. At the beginning of the year, people say "_____!"
    a) **Happy New Year**
    b) **Good New Year**
    c) **Happy Year**

241. "Oh, how we danced on the night we were wed" is the beginning of _____.
    a) **The Anniversary Waltz**
    b) **The Blue Danube Waltz**
    c) **The Tennessee Waltz**

242. An **engagement party** is for two people who are going to _____.
    a) start a business
    b) get married
    c) enter the army

243. On **national holidays** people never _____.
    a) go shopping
    b) travel to Great Britain
    c) receive mail

244. People bring their best homemade pies and fattest cows for judging at _____.
    a) **company picnics**
    b) **anniversary parties**
    c) **county fairs**

245. Flower shops are busiest on **Valentine's Day** and _____.
    a) **Father's Day**
    b) **Mother's Day**
    c) **Thanksgiving Day**

246. The theme of a **Valentine's party** is _____.
    a) travel
    b) food
    c) love

247. **Witches**, **ghosts** and **goblins** appear on _____.
    a) October 31
    b) December 31
    c) May 30

248. **Mother's Day** is on the second Sunday in _____.
    a) May
    b) June
    c) July

249. When two people **plan to marry**, the man often gives the woman a _____.
    a) gold necklace
    b) silver bracelet
    c) diamond ring

250. On a **bank holiday** _____.
    a) people receive free calendars at the bank
    b) bankers have a party for rich customers
    c) banks close for the day

Vocabulary

PART ONE

H_2O

H_2O

H_2O

gobble, gobble...bow wow...quack, quack... bow wow...go

Directions: Complete the sentences.

251. People cook in the _____.
    a) **chicken**
    b) **dining room**
    c) **kitchen**

252. What do you wear around your wrist that tells time? A _____.
    a) **clock**
    b) **watch**
    c) **bracelet**

253. People have ten fingers on their hands. On their feet they have ten _____.
    a) **thumbs**
    b) **fingers**
    c) **toes**

254. What do people wear around their neck to keep warm? A _____.
   a) **scarf**
   b) **necklace**
   c) **tie**

255. A woman who is going to have a baby is _____.
   a) **plural**
   b) **pregnant**
   c) **pink**

256. Your sister or brother's daughter is your _____.
   a) **niece**
   b) **nephew**
   c) **cousin**

257. To **pass** a test is to _____.
   a) take it
   b) do well
   c) fail it

258. A **library** is the place where you _____.
   a) buy books
   b) borrow books
   c) sell books

259. Your home is the place where you _____.
   a) **live**
   b) **leave**
   c) **sightsee**

260. You have a dollar, but need pennies, nickels, dimes and quarters. You want _____.
   a) **change**
   b) **bills**
   c) **small money**

261. Coats are made in a _____.
   a) **fabric**
   b) **field**
   c) **factory**

262. Your **parents** are your _____.
   a) cousins, aunts and uncles
   b) sisters and brothers
   c) mother and father

263. Doctors, nurses, policemen, firemen and soldiers wear _____.
   a) **medals**
   b) **uniforms**
   c) **suits**

264. A **skyscraper** is another name for _____.
    a) a cloud
    b) an airplane
    c) a tall building

265. The people who live near you are your _____.
    a) **neighbors**
    b) **relatives**
    c) **friends**

266. After a bath you dry yourself with a _____.
    a) **napkin**
    b) **towel**
    c) **tissue**

267. You can see yourself best in a _____.
    a) **window**
    b) **glass**
    c) **mirror**

268. People wash with _____.
    a) **soup and water**
    b) **soap and water**
    c) **snow and water**

269. Animals you keep in your home are called _____.
    a) **pets**
    b) **pests**
    c) **pens**

270. People who smoke use _____.
    a) **a cup**
    b) **an ashtray**
    c) **a pan**

271. You drink water when you are _____.
    a) **thirty**
    b) **hungry**
    c) **thirsty**

272. When you don't understand a word, you use _____.
    a) **a dictionary**
    b) **an encyclopedia**
    c) **a map**

273. The opposite of **near** is _____.
    a) **far from**
    b) **between**
    c) **away**

274. Lipstick, powder and blush are _____.
    a) **make-up**
    b) **covers**
    c) **paint**

275. A person who is very sick goes to a _____.
    a) **motel**
    b) **hotel**
    c) **hospital**

276. A **handsome** man is _____.
    a) good-looking
    b) nice
    c) smart

277. There is a lot of traffic. Traffic is _____.
    a) **big**
    b) **full**
    c) **heavy**

278. Cows live in _____.
    a) **nests**
    b) **barns**
    c) **parks**

279. At the end of a concert or play, people _____.
    a) **nap**
    b) **clap**
    c) **chat**

280. You go to a barber for a _____.
    a) **haircut**
    b) **beer**
    c) **barbeque**

281. If you are not married, you are _____.
    a) **free**
    b) **lonely**
    c) **single**

282. Between your house and the house next door, you can build a _____.
    a) **fence**
    b) **curtain**
    c) **door**

283. The opposite of **north** is _____.
    a) **west**
    b) **east**
    c) **south**

284. People keep cars in a _____.
    a) **garden**
    b) **garage**
    c) **yard**

285. **Almost** an hour is a little _____.
    a) less than an hour
    b) more than an hour
    c) more or less than an hour

286. The opposite of the **floor** is the _____.
    a) **wall**
    b) **sky**
    c) **ceiling**

287. You know your friend has worked hard preparing a meal for you. You say, "The food is _____."
    a) **nice**
    b) **OK**
    c) **delicious**

288. In the United States, young children often call their mothers, "_____."
    a) **Mother**
    b) **Mommy**
    c) **Mum**

289. Women often wear a **blouse** with a _____.
    a) shirt
    b) skirt
    c) dress

290. H_2O is _____.
    a) water
    b) salt
    c) air

291. Cups, saucers and plates are _____.
    a) **food**
    b) **appliances**
    c) **dishes**

292. There are 365 days in a _____.
    a) **month**
    b) **year**
    c) **decade**

293. When people sleep, they _____.
    a) **yawn**
    b) **blush**
    c) **dream**

294. You want to hang a picture on the wall so you use a nail and a _____.
    a) **hammer**
    b) **saw**
    c) **scale**

295. **Sugar** is _____.
    a) sweet
    b) sour
    c) salty

296. A **restaurant** is a place to _____.
    a) rest
    b) eat
    c) sleep

297. Lemons taste _____.
    a) **sweet**
    b) **sour**
    c) **salty**

298. When you order food in a restaurant, you ask to see the _____.
    a) **menu**
    b) **list**
    c) **chart**

299. A rose _____.
    a) **smells** good
    b) **tastes** good
    c) **sounds** good

300. A **busboy** works _____.
    a) on a bus
    b) in a restaurant
    c) in a bus factory

301. The name of a book is its _____.
    a) **contents**
    b) **page**
    c) **title**

302. The opposite of a **winner** is a _____.
    a) **thief**
    b) **loser**
    c) **stranger**

303. You want to leave. You look for a sign that says _____.
    a) **Exit**
    b) **Men's**
    c) **Go**

304. People work at their _____.
    a) **dressers**
    b) **desks**
    c) **closets**

305. Breakfast, lunch and dinner are _____.
    a) **food**
    b) **meals**
    c) **snacks**

306. A **century** is one hundred _____.
    a) dollars
    b) people
    c) years

307. **Lettuce** is _____.
    a) a fruit
    b) a vegetable
    c) an animal

308. An **infant** is a _____.
    a) child
    b) baby
    c) soldier

309. The opposite of **upstairs** is _____.
    a) **downstairs**
    b) **outside**
    c) **behind**

310. Pineapples, grapes and plums are _____.
    a) **fruit**
    b) **vegetables**
    c) **flowers**

311. We eat on a _____.
    a) **cup**
    b) **pillow**
    c) **plate**

312. The opposite of **above** is _____.
    a) **below**
    b) **between**
    c) **into**

313. Many women and some men decorate their ears with _____.
    a) **ear plugs**
    b) **hearing aids**
    c) **earrings**

314. You can't eat anymore. You feel _____.
    a) **clean**
    b) **full**
    c) **fed**

315. When it's raining and you don't want to get wet, you use _____.
    a) **a parachute**
    b) **a dryer**
    c) **an umbrella**

316. Children play in a _____.
    a) **sandwich**
    b) **sandal**
    c) **sandbox**

317. People eat when they feel _____.
    a) **hungry**
    b) **angry**
    c) **thirsty**

318. A person who sells meat is called a _____.
    a) **barber**
    b) **farmer**
    c) **butcher**

319. When you get hurt, you say "_____!"
    a) **Wee**
    b) **Ha**
    c) **Ouch**

320. We cut meat with a fork and _____.
    a) **sword**
    b) **knife**
    c) **spoon**

321. A **deaf** person cannot _____.
    a) see
    b) breathe
    c) hear

322. Ducks say "_____."
    a) **Gobble, gobble**
    b) **Bow, wow**
    c) **Quack, quack**

323. Aristotle Onassis was Jacqueline Kennedy's _____.
    a) **second** husband
    b) **two** husband
    c) **twice** husband

324. I'm sorry I'm late. I _____.
   a) **lost** my bus
   b) **missed** my bus
   c) **left** my bus

325. Last weekend we _____.
   a) **moved** into a new apartment
   b) **changed** into a new apartment
   c) **removed** into a new apartment

326. The opposite of **always** is _____.
   a) **sometimes**
   b) **occasionally**
   c) **never**

327. The opposite of **early** is _____.
   a) **tomorrow**
   b) **late**
   c) **soon**

328. You want to watch a TV show so you turn to the right _____.
   a) **channel**
   b) **dial**
   c) **switch**

329. A doctor who takes care of teeth is called a _____.
   a) **druggist**
   b) **dentist**
   c) **dragon**

330. The opposite of **tiny** is _____.
   a) **thin**
   b) **huge**
   c) **little**

331. An **architect** is a person who designs _____.
   a) clothes
   b) houses
   c) jewelry

332. When people speak a language you don't know, you can't _____.
   a) **hear** them
   b) **listen to** them
   c) **understand** them

333. The opposite of the **future** is the _____.
   a) **past**
   b) **present**
   c) **morning**

American History, Geography and Government

PART ONE

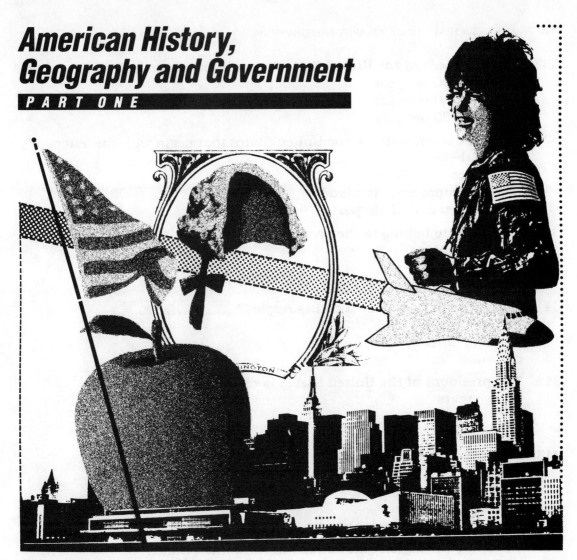

Directions: Complete the sentences.

334. What bird is the **symbol of the United States**? The _____.
    a) turkey
    b) eagle
    c) owl

335. The **American Civil War** was a war between the _____.
    a) North and the South
    b) East and the West
    c) United States and Great Britain

336. What is "**The Star-Spangled Banner**"? _____.
    a) a song from *Star Wars*
    b) an American football song
    c) the National Anthem

337. **How many states** are there in the United States today? _____.
    a) 50
    b) 48
    c) 52

338. **The president of the United States earns** about _____.
    a) $100,000 per year
    b) $200,000 per year
    c) $500,000 per year

339. There are seven states in the United States that begin with the letter "m". Two of them are _____.
    a) **Mexico** and **Maine**
    b) **Mississippi** and **Maryland**
    c) **Madison** and **Michigan**

340. When we are talking to the president, we call him, "_____."
    a) **President**
    b) **Your Majesty**
    c) **Mr. President**

341. Which city is known as "**The Big Apple**"? _____.
    a) New York City
    b) San Francisco
    c) Dallas

342. **The president of the United States is elected** for _____.
    a) two years
    b) four years
    c) six years

343. The **first woman** to run for vice president of the United States was _____.
    a) Jeane Kirkpatrick
    b) Geraldine Ferraro
    c) Jacqueline Kennedy Onassis

344. Where are the **highest mountains** in the United States? In the _____.
    a) South
    b) Northeast
    c) West

345. **Uncle Sam** is another name for _____.
    a) the United States government
    b) Samuel Morse
    c) George Washington's brother

346. What is **the capital** of the United States? _____.
    a) Washington
    b) Washington, D.C.
    c) New York

347. The **longest river** in the United States is the _____.
    a) Hudson River
    b) Mississippi River
    c) Delaware River

348. **Cowboys** live in the _____.
   a) West
   b) East
   c) Midwest

349. The president of the United States lives in the _____.
   a) **Green House**
   b) **Gold House**
   c) **White House**

350. **Disney World** is in _____.
   a) Detroit
   b) San Francisco
   c) Orlando

351. Which state has the **smallest population**? _____.
   a) Alaska
   b) Ohio
   c) Rhode Island

352. The only president of the United States elected for four terms was _____.
   a) **Franklin D. Roosevelt**
   b) **Abraham Lincoln**
   c) **John F. Kennedy**

353. The **population** of the United States is about _____.
   a) 240 million
   b) 140 million
   c) 340 million

354. Which American president had the nickname "**Honest Abe**"? _____.
   a) Madison
   b) Nixon
   c) Lincoln

355. In 1971 the **voting age** was lowered from 21 to _____.
   a) 19 years
   b) 18 years
   c) 17 years

356. **George Washington**, like many men in the 1700s, wore _____.
   a) a wig
   b) jeans
   c) earrings

357. Which of the following is not a state? _____.
   a) **Oklahoma**
   b) **Alabama**
   c) **Washington, D.C.**

358. **Neil Armstrong** was the first American to _____.
    a) visit Alaska
    b) land on the moon
    c) discover gold in California

359. If a United States **president dies**, _____.
    a) the vice president becomes the president
    b) there is a new election
    c) the president's wife becomes the president

360. The **first English colony** in the New World was founded in 1607 in _____.
    a) Massachusetts
    b) Maryland
    c) Virginia

361. **The Golden Gate Bridge** is in _____.
    a) San Francisco
    b) San Diego
    c) San Jose

362. **The president of the United States** must be at least _____.
    a) thirty-five years old
    b) forty years old
    c) forty-five years old

363. How many **major political parties** are there in the United States today? _____.
    a) three
    b) ten
    c) two

364. **The Windy City** is another name for _____.
    a) Detroit
    b) Chicago
    c) Tulsa

365. The **American flag** has _____.
    a) a sun, a moon and stars
    b) a maple leaf
    c) stars and stripes

366. What is the **automobile capital** of America? _____.
    a) Chicago
    b) Detroit
    c) Mobile

367. "**In God We Trust**" is printed on all United States _____.
    a) money
    b) post offices
    c) military uniforms

368. The **highest court** in the United States is the _____.
    a) Supreme Court
    b) High Court
    c) Supreme Council

369. The only father and son who were presidents of the United States
    were the _____.
    a) **Roosevelts**
    b) **Kennedys**
    c) **Adams**

370. **The Alamo** is in _____.
    a) New Mexico
    b) Texas
    c) Alabama

371. **San Francisco** is famous for its _____.
    a) horse and buggy rides
    b) buses
    c) cable cars

372. The **desert areas** of the United States are in the _____.
    a) East
    b) West
    c) Midwest

373. In the United States, the **wife of the president** is called _____.
    a) the first woman
    b) the first wife
    c) the first lady

374. The city best known for **gambling** is _____.
    a) Las Vegas
    b) Los Angeles
    c) Miami Beach

375. What city has **the most people**? _____.
    a) Dallas
    b) New York
    c) Chicago

376. The United States bought **Florida** from _____. *Dimitriy*
    a) Holland
    b) Mexico
    c) Spain

377. **Daniel Boone** and **Davy Crockett** were famous American _____.
    a) pioneers
    b) generals
    c) cowboys

378. **Sally Ride** and **John Glenn** are famous American _____
    a) diplomats
    b) astronauts
    c) mayors

379. On **November 22, 1963** _____.
    a) the first Americans landed on the moon
    b) John F. Kennedy was killed
    c) the Vietnam War began

380. **Denver** is the capital of _____.
    a) Colorado
    b) California
    c) Oregon

381. When **John F. Kennedy** became president, he was _____.
    a) 43 years old
    b) 54 years old
    c) 34 years old

382. On every **one dollar bill**, there's a picture of _____.
    a) Abraham Lincoln
    b) George Washington
    c) John Adams

383. The **highest mountain** in the United States is _____.
    a) Mt. Washington, in New Hampshire
    b) Mt. Rushmore, in South Dakota
    c) Mt. McKinley, in Alaska

384. The **people** in each state **elect** _____.
    a) two U.S. senators
    b) four U.S. senators
    c) one U.S. senator

385. In **1849** people rushed to California to find _____.
    a) oil
    b) silver
    c) gold

386. Before you can **become an American citizen**, you must have lived in the United States at least _____.
    a) one year
    b) five years
    c) eight years

387. Before **Ronald Reagan** became a politican, he was _____.
    a) a lawyer
    b) a soldier
    c) an actor

388. **Gold** is kept in _____.
  a) Fort Knox, Kentucky
  b) Fort Dix, New Jersey
  c) Fort Worth, Texas

389. The **cherry blossoms** in Washington, D.C. were a gift to the United States from _____.
  a) Canada
  b) Japan
  c) Holland

390. There was a big **earthquake** in 1906 in _____.
  a) Dallas, Texas
  b) San Francisco, California
  c) Seattle, Washington

391. Most **oranges** in the United States come from _____.
  a) California and Florida
  b) Arizona and Nevada
  c) Texas and New Mexico

392. **The Liberty Bell** is in _____.
  a) New York
  b) Boston
  c) Philadelphia

393. In what part of the United States is most of the **cotton and tobacco** grown? In the _____.
  a) West
  b) Midwest
  c) South

394. Each state has a _____.
  a) **mayor**
  b) **governor**
  c) **major**

395. **The Grand Canyon** is in the _____.
  a) East
  b) South
  c) West

396. **The Statue of Liberty** was a gift from _____.
  a) Liberia
  b) Holland
  c) France

397. **Cowboy hats and boots** are often seen in _____.
  a) New Jersey
  b) Texas
  c) Connecticut

398. **Alcatraz** used to be a large _____.
    a) hotel
    b) prison
    c) school

399. Every big city has a _____.
    a) **senator**
    b) **mayor**
    c) **director**

400. **America** was named after _____.
    a) the Amerindian
    b) Amerigo Vespucci
    c) a merit system

401. **Buffalo Bill** was famous for his _____.
    a) meat business
    b) clothing business
    c) Wild West shows

402. The **Indian princess** who helped the colonists at Jamestown, Virginia was _____.
    a) Pocahontas
    b) Leah Organa
    c) Isabelle

403. The **least crowded state** in the United States is _____.
    a) Rhode Island
    b) Alaska
    c) Hawaii

404. Many people work in the **coal mines** of _____.
    a) Kentucky, West Virginia and Pennsylvania
    b) California, Washington and Oregon
    c) Michigan, Wisconsin and Illinois

405. Most **potatoes** are grown in _____.
    a) Idaho
    b) Florida
    c) Texas

406. Which state has been called **the Last Frontier**? _____.
    a) California
    b) Texas
    c) Alaska

407. **The Empire State** is another name for _____.
    a) New York
    b) Illinois
    c) Massachusetts

408. Which of the following is not an island? _____.
    a) **Manhattan**
    b) **Hawaii**
    c) **Rhode Island**

409. Today nobody can be **elected president** more than _____.
    a) once
    b) twice
    c) three times

410. **The Sunshine State** is another name for _____.
    a) New Mexico
    b) Florida
    c) Alabama

411. Many astronauts work for _____.
    a) **NASA**
    b) **NATO**
    c) **Nabisco**

412. The **Indians** taught the Pilgrims how to grow _____.
    a) rice
    b) tulips
    c) corn

413. In what year did **Christopher Columbus** reach the New World? _____.
    a) 1492
    b) 1607
    c) 1776

414. In 1620 the Pilgrims landed in Massachusetts. The name of their ship was the _____.
    a) **Nina**
    b) **Half Moon**
    c) **Mayflower**

415. The United States bought **Alaska** from _____.
    a) Canada
    b) Russia
    c) Spain

416. Four states begin with the word **New**. They are New York, New Mexico, New Hampshire and New _____.
    a) London
    b) Brunswick
    c) Jersey

417. Each star on the **American flag** represents a _____.
    a) president
    b) region
    c) state

Grammar

PART ONE

Directions: Complete the sentences.

418. Tokyo is _____.
    a) a capital of Japan
    b) capital of Japan
    c) the capital of Japan

419. He needs a dollar _____.
    a) to buy a pen
    b) for to buy a pen
    c) for buy a pen

420. I'm wearing a sweater and a jacket because _____.
    a) I'm cold
    b) I have cold
    c) I cold

421. Caroline doesn't type and _____.
    a) Ray doesn't, too
    b) Ray does, too
    c) Ray doesn't, either

422. He lives _____.
    a) on third floor
    b) on the third floor
    c) on the three floor

423. Kate goes to school _____.
    a) by bus
    b) on bus
    c) in bus

424. Frank doesn't have many girlfriends, _____?
    a) does he
    b) did he
    c) hasn't he

425. February is _____.
    a) the most shortest month of the year
    b) the shortest month of the year
    c) the most short month of the year

426. Every morning Karen walks _____.
    a) to work
    b) by work
    c) onto work

427. After the movie Russell and Andrea walked _____.
    a) to home
    b) home
    c) in home

428. Send _____.
    a) her my love
    b) to her my love
    c) it to her my love

429. He painted that house, _____?
    a) doesn't he
    b) didn't he
    c) did he

430. My boss is _____.
    a) at vacation
    b) in vacation
    c) on vacation

431. Dr. and Mrs. Kissinger are going to Hawaii _____.
     a) to one week
     b) for one week
     c) during one week

432. Her children _____.
     a) doesn't like vegetables
     b) no like vegetables
     c) don't like vegetables

433. I'd like _____.
     a) some milk for my coffee
     b) a milk for my coffee
     c) any milk for my coffee

434. In the future people _____.
     a) are going to have more free time
     b) going to have more free time
     c) going have more free time

435. I live on Twenty-third Street _____.
     a) between Main and Church
     b) on Main and Church
     c) next to Main and Church

436. I'd like a cup _____.
     a) coffee
     b) of coffee
     c) with coffee

437. There weren't _____.
     a) some eggs in the refrigerator
     b) an egg in the refrigerator
     c) any eggs in the refrigerator

438. Every evening Bernie and Lenore listen _____.
     a) classical music
     b) to classical music
     c) on classical music

439. That yellow and orange tie _____.
     a) cost me twenty dollars
     b) cost twenty dollars to me
     c) cost twenty dollars for me

440. This plate is clean but those _____.
     a) cups is dirty
     b) cup is dirty
     c) cups are dirty

441. The teacher said, "_____!"
    a) You don't open your books
    b) Don't open your books
    c) Not to open your books

442. We don't want _____.
    a) no pepper
    b) any pepper
    c) some pepper

443. Half past eight is the same as _____.
    a) eight-fifteen
    b) eight-thirty
    c) eight o'clock

444. I don't believe _____.
    a) her
    b) she
    c) hers

445. Please give me _____.
    a) any money
    b) some money
    c) a money

446. How many songs _____?
    a) sang Michael Jackson
    b) did Michael Jackson sang
    c) did Michael Jackson sing

447. I bought an expensive camera, but _____.
    a) a camera never worked
    b) camera never worked
    c) the camera never worked

448. We can see _____.
    a) the Pacific Ocean from our hotel room
    b) a Pacific Ocean from our hotel room
    c) Pacific Ocean from our hotel room

449. The waitress asked, "_____?"
    a) What would you like to drink
    b) What will you like to drink
    c) What do you like to drink

450. This restaurant is even _____.
    a) more bad than the other
    b) worse than the other
    c) worst than the other

Directions: Answer the questions.

451. What's the weather like?
    a) I like it hot.
    b) It's hot.
    c) I feel hot.

452. How old is Dahlia?
    a) She has eight.
    b) She eight.
    c) She's eight.

453. What does she do?
    a) She's a lawyer.
    b) She's lawyer.
    c) She a lawyer.

454. What are the children doing?
    a) They're playing ball outside.
    b) They play ball outside.
    c) They playing ball outside.

455. Are you a student?
    a) Yes, I'm.
    b) Yes, I am.
    c) Yes, I'm student.

456. When did Pedro go to Miami?
    a) Before two months.
    b) Two months before.
    c) Two months ago.

457. What's today's date?
    a) It April twenty-fourth.
    b) It's April twenty-fourth.
    c) It's twenty-four April.

458. How much coffee do you want?
    a) A lot of.
    b) A lot.
    c) Lots of.

459. Do you live in an apartment?
    a) Yes, I do.
    b) Yes, I am.
    c) Yes, I live.

460. Which is more expensive, a motorcycle or a bicycle?
    a) A motorcycle is more expensive a bicycle.
    b) A motorcycle is more expensive that a bicycle.
    c) A motorcycle is more expensive than a bicycle.

461. When did the Millers come to New York?
     a) They arrived New York in 1985.
     b) They arrived at New York in 1985.
     c) They arrived in New York in 1985.

462. Why did you buy a new watch?
     a) This one is better that my old one.
     b) This one is better than my old one.
     c) This one is better as my old one.

463. Who's in Italy?
     a) The father my friend.
     b) My friend father.
     c) My friend's father.

464. Whose book is this?
     a) It belongs to him.
     b) It belongs to his.
     c) It belongs to he.

465. Where do Marty and Diane live?
     a) In 345 East 85th Street.
     b) On 345 East 85th Street.
     c) At 345 East 85th Street.

466. Do you like your teacher?
     a) Of course, I like.
     b) Of course, I do.
     c) Of course, I am.

467. Where do you live?
     a) In the new, red building.
     b) In the new building red.
     c) In the building new and red.

468. Where's the rest of the cake?
     a) Me and Andrea ate it.
     b) I and Andrea ate it.
     c) Andrea and I ate it.

469. Where is Jack going?
     a) He's going to take home her.
     b) He's going to take her home.
     c) He's going to take she home.

470. Did you eat alone?
     a) No, I ate Rita and Paul.
     b) No, I ate for Rita and Paul.
     c) No, I ate with Rita and Paul.

471. Where are your seats?
    a) In the five row.
    b) In the row five.
    c) In the fifth row.

472. How much money did you bring with you?
    a) I brought ten dollars.
    b) I bought ten dollars.
    c) I bring ten dollars.

473. Where's Bella's hat?
    a) She's here.
    b) It's here.
    c) Its here.

474. Where's your aunt?
    a) He's over there.
    b) Hers is over there.
    c) She's over there.

475. What did Seiji Ozawa do last night?
    a) He went to a concert.
    b) He goes to a concert.
    c) He did go to a concert.

476. Are the new secretaries working hard?
    a) Yes, they do.
    b) Yes, they are.
    c) Yes, they will.

477. Why are you so late?
    a) I didn't woke up on time.
    b) I didn't wake up on time.
    c) I not wake up on time.

478. Are you ready to order?
    a) Yes, we are.
    b) Yes, we order.
    c) Yes, we ready.

479. What does she do on Sundays?
    a) She usually is going to church.
    b) She usually goes to church.
    c) She usually went to church.

480. Did they catch that fish or buy it?
    a) They catch it.
    b) They did catch it.
    c) They caught it.

481. Does Mr. Steiner attend every meeting?
    a) No, he always doesn't go.
    b) No, he doesn't always go.
    c) No, he doesn't go always.

Directions: Read the first sentence in each item. Then choose the correct second sentence.

482. I only have ten dollars.
    a) How much moneys do we need?
    b) How much money do we need?
    c) How many money do we need?

483. Pamela's going to a party.
    a) She wants new dress.
    b) She wants some new dress.
    c) She wants a new dress.

484. I forgot my wallet.
    a) May I borrow any money?
    b) May I borrow some money?
    c) May I borrow a few money?

485. I'm not hungry.
    a) I don't want no rice.
    b) I don't want any rice.
    c) I don't want a rice.

486. I can't decide right now.
    a) I need a little time.
    b) I need a few time.
    c) I need many time.

487. These letters are Uncle Oscar's.
    a) Please give them to him.
    b) Please give them to her.
    c) Please give it to him.

488. Hal is becoming a good ice skater.
    a) Every Wednesday he is taking ice skating lessons.
    b) Every Wednesday he takes ice skating lessons.
    c) Every Wednesday he is taken ice skating lessons.

489. Deborah doesn't speak Italian.
    a) Cynthia doesn't, too.
    b) Cynthia doesn't, either.
    c) Cynthia doesn't, neither.

490. George knows shorthand.
    a) Can he to type, too?
    b) Can he types, too?
    c) Can he type, too?

491. You are carrying a lot of magazines.
    a) Where did you get it?
    b) Where did you get they?
    c) Where did you get them?

492. They all feel sick.
    a) What did they ate for breakfast?
    b) What did they eat for breakfast?
    c) What did they eats for breakfast?

493. You look tired.
    a) Would you like to stop and rest?
    b) Will you like to stop and rest?
    c) Do you like to stop and rest?

494. That hat isn't yours.
    a) It's my.
    b) It's me.
    c) It's mine.

495. There's going to be an important meeting next Monday.
    a) I hope to see you there.
    b) I will hope to see you there.
    c) I am hope to see you there.

496. I like this restaurant.
    a) There are always little people here.
    b) There are always few people here.
    c) There are always a little people here.

497. Your class is in room 340.
    a) Ours is in room 240.
    b) We is in room 240.
    c) Our is in room 240.

498. I didn't see you at the office yesterday.
    a) Where was you?
    b) Where were you?
    c) Where did you be?

499. Johnny broke a lamp.
    a) Which one did he break?
    b) Which one did he broke?
    c) Which one broke he?

500. Whose key is that?
    a) They're hers.
    b) They're her.
    c) It's hers.

General Knowledge about the United States

PART TWO

March comes in like a

Directions: Complete the sentences.

501. A child of three or four attends a _____.
- a) **nursery school**
- b) **nursing school**
- c) **nursing home**

502. A person gets a **bachelor's degree** _____.
- a) on the day after a divorce
- b) after finishing college
- c) on the day before a marriage

503. People with **spring fever** _____.
- a) need a medical doctor
- b) need aspirin and bed rest
- c) need a vacation

504. **Love** is worth nothing in _____.
- a) marriage
- b) life
- c) tennis

505. What is a **baby shower**? It's a _____.
   a) party for a woman who is going to have a baby
   b) place where babies are washed
   c) small amount of rain

506. A widow is a woman whose husband has died. A **football widow** is a woman whose husband _____.
   a) died playing football
   b) watches football games all weekend
   c) is a professional football player

507. **To join the army**, you have to _____.
   a) have a high school diploma
   b) have your parents' permission
   c) be eighteen years old

508. On every **one dollar bill** there is a picture of _____.
   a) a pyramid
   b) a cave
   c) a tent

509. **To get a waiter's attention**, you should not _____.
   a) raise your hand
   b) wait for him to look at you
   c) clap your hands

510. **Outstanding baseball players** are elected to _____.
   a) Yankee Stadium
   b) the U.S. Senate
   c) the Baseball Hall of Fame

511. Someone going to an **out-of-town college** is going to a college _____.
   a) in the country
   b) on a farm
   c) away from home

512. A **strike** is always good for _____.
   a) baseball players
   b) bowlers
   c) workers

513. Because hospitals are very expensive, most **people who get sick** _____.
   a) eat health food
   b) go to another country
   c) have health insurance

514. When a friend invites you to a **potluck** dinner, you bring _____.
   a) food
   b) flowers
   c) a present

515. **Hard rock**, **heavy metal** and **reggae** are kinds of _____.
   a) music
   b) furniture
   c) jewelry

516. **William Faulkner**, **Ernest Hemingway** and **John Steinbeck** were famous American _____.
   a) writers
   b) painters
   c) musicians

517. A **delivery room** is the place where _____.
   a) mail is separated
   b) babies are born
   c) newspapers are printed

518. At a **garage sale** you can buy _____.
   a) automobile parts
   b) many different things
   c) garages

519. You wouldn't write to a friend in the hospital, "_____."
   a) **I wish you a speedy recovery**
   b) **Get well soon**
   c) **Good luck in your new location**

520. When writing a **business letter** to your lawyer, Ellen Lehrer, you begin, _____.
   a) My Dear Ellen:
   b) Dearest Ms. Lehrer:
   c) Dear Ms. Lehrer:

521. There is a saying, "**March comes in like a lion and goes out like a _____.**"
   a) lamb
   b) lady
   c) lover

522. A **Ph.D.** can use the title _____.
   a) Doctor
   b) Reverend
   c) Judge

523. **Annie Oakley** was known for her ability to use a _____.
   a) pen
   b) paintbrush
   c) gun

524. She was blind and deaf but with the help of a special teacher, she became a great writer. Her name was _____.
   a) **Anne Sullivan**
   b) **Helen Keller**
   c) **Hester Prynne**

525. Your friend invited you to join her for **dinner at seven o'clock.** You arrived at eight o'clock. You arrived _____.
   a) very late and should apologize
   b) a little late but you don't have to apologize
   c) on time

526. The **first American college** opened in 1636. This college, which is still very important today, is called _____.
   a) Harvard
   b) Stanford
   c) Columbia

527. This newspaper first appeared in 1851. It carried the words that are still on its front page, "All the News that's Fit to Print." This newspaper is _____.
   a) **The Los Angeles Times**
   b) **The Washington Post**
   c) **The New York Times**

528. Many people dislike **April 15** because it is the day _____.
   a) people must pay taxes
   b) prisoners can leave jail
   c) students have to take exams

529. The **ASPCA** helps _____.
   a) actresses and actors
   b) athletes
   c) animals

530. **Public schools** in the United States are _____.
   a) free for all
   b) $1,000 a year
   c) 10% of a family's income

531. You were invited to **a big party** that began at eight-thirty. You came at nine o'clock. You arrived _____.
   a) very late and should apologize
   b) a little late, but you don't have to apologize
   c) too early. Parties never get going until eleven o'clock.

532. People who work in the **stock market** buy and sell _____.
   a) cattle
   b) stockings
   c) shares in businesses

533. In the United States it is very **rude** to _____.
   a) walk along the street eating ice cream
   b) have a conversation during a meal
   c) spit on the street

534. **Billy the Kid** was a famous _____.
   a) circus goat
   b) child actor
   c) outlaw

535. Harvard, Princeton, Yale, Columbia, Dartmouth, Brown, Cornell and the University of Pennsylvania are _____.
    a) **Ivory Tower Colleges**
    b) **Ivy League Colleges**
    c) **Little League Colleges**

536. **Susan B. Anthony** worked to help _____.
    a) children
    b) women
    c) immigrants

537. One of the most famous mothers in the United States was _____.
    a) **Washington's mother**
    b) **Franklin Roosevelt's mother**
    c) **Whistler's mother**

538. **Samuel Clemens** wrote *Huckleberry Finn* and *Tom Sawyer*. He is also known as _____.
    a) Mark Twain
    b) Ernest Hemingway
    c) James Fenimore Cooper

539. **Grandma Moses** and **Jackson Pollack** were famous American _____.
    a) rock singers
    b) painters
    c) philosophers

540. If you hear, "The **Indians killed the Yankees** yesterday in New York City," you _____.
    a) stay away from New York
    b) ask about the baseball game
    c) learn sign language

541. People get **social security** _____.
    a) when they retire
    b) on a vacation
    c) from the police

542. The **Harlem Globetrotters** are _____.
    a) a travel agency
    b) a jogging team
    c) a basketball team

543. What kind of dance began in the United States? The _____.
    a) **Square Dance**
    b) **Line Dance**
    c) **Circle Dance**

544. In American football the players can **move the ball** with _____.
    a) their hands
    b) their heads
    c) their teeth

545. If you **leave your shoes** outside your hotel room in the United States, _____.
    a) someone will polish them
    b) someone will throw them away
    c) nobody will polish them

546. People ask for a **doggy bag** _____.
    a) at a pet shop
    b) at a restaurant
    c) at a zoo

547. Chico, Groucho, Harpo and Zeppo were the first names of the _____.
    a) **Wright Brothers**
    b) **Marx Brothers**
    c) **Smothers Brothers**

548. If you **find $1,000** and give it to the police, _____.
    a) you get $100 reward
    b) you never receive a reward
    c) you may or may not receive a reward

549. A man uses "**Jr.**" after his name if he _____.
    a) is under 21 years old
    b) is in school
    c) has the same name as his father

550. **Normal body temperature** is 37 degrees Centigrade or _____.
    a) 89.6 degrees Fahrenheit
    b) 98.6 degrees Fahrenheit
    c) 100 degrees Fahrenheit

551. What kind of music started in the South in the early 1900s? _____.
    a) **Jazz**
    b) **Country Western**
    c) **Rock 'n Roll**

552. A speed limit of **55 miles per hour** is the same as _____.
    a) 88 kilometers per hour
    b) 48 kilometers per hour
    c) 100 kilometers per hour

553. When you **dial the wrong number**, you _____.
    a) hang up immediately
    b) say, "Excuse me. I must have dialed the wrong number"
    c) ask for the name and address of the person you reach

554. An **Oscar** is an award for a _____.
    a) movie
    b) TV show
    c) book

555. People put **French**, **Italian** and **Russian dressing** on their _____.
    a) body
    b) food
    c) cuts

556. When a family says **grace** before a meal, the family is _____.
    a) saying a prayer
    b) playing a game
    c) singing a song

557. A **B.L.T.** is a _____.
    a) subway train
    b) sandwich
    c) basketball team

558. **ID cards** are for _____.
    a) inexperienced drivers
    b) identification
    c) eye doctors

559. People in the Northeast talk about **Indian Summer** on a hot day in the _____.
    a) spring
    b) summer
    c) fall

560. A **rodeo** is a _____.
    a) radio with earphones
    b) cowboy show
    c) horse race

561. **Bob Dylan** and **Joan Baez** are famous American _____.
    a) folk singers
    b) opera singers
    c) rock singers

562. Some people think **a rabbit's foot** brings _____.
    a) trouble
    b) good luck
    c) many children

563. What sports event takes place in a ring? _____.
    a) **tennis**
    b) **football**
    c) **boxing**

564. **Frank Lloyd Wright** was a famous _____.
    a) architect
    b) lawyer
    c) writer

565. **Al Capone** was a _____.
   a) painter
   b) lawyer
   c) gangster

566. **Most Americans sleep** _____.
   a) an hour after lunch
   b) only at night
   c) two hours every afternoon

567. On the **last Sunday in October**, people move their clocks one hour
   _____.
   a) back
   b) ahead
   c) neither

568. Before each **Major League baseball game**, the audience stands and
   sings _____.
   a) "Happy Days Are Here Again"
   b) "Take Me Out to the Ball Game"
   c) "The Star-Spangled Banner"

569. People who want to know about babies get a book by _____.
   a) **Benjamin Moore**
   b) **Benjamin Franklin**
   c) **Benjamin Spock**

570. **Courts** are for judges and _____.
   a) tennis players
   b) card players
   c) ping-pong players

571. **Hearts, Diamonds, Spades** and **Clubs** are types of _____.
   a) candy
   b) cards
   c) jewelry

572. "**Porgy and Bess**" was written by _____.
   a) George Gershwin
   b) Harry Belafonte
   c) Oscar Hammerstein

573. Many people in the United States eat _____.
   a) **rice** at every meal
   b) **corn** at every meal
   c) **bread** at every meal

574. **Eric Severeid, Barbara Walters** and **Dan Rather** talk about _____.
   a) the news
   b) the weather
   c) sports

575. When you throw a coin in the air, you call **heads** or _____.
   a) **feet**
   b) **tails**
   c) **toes**

576. **Rush hour** is usually between seven and nine o'clock in the morning and _____.
   a) three and five o'clock in the afternoon
   b) five and seven o'clock in the evening
   c) seven and nine o'clock at night

577. **Robert Frost** and **Emily Dickenson** were _____.
   a) poets
   b) sculptors
   c) politicians

578. In 1975 the Federal government lowered the **speed limit** to _____.
   a) 45 miles per hour
   b) 55 miles per hour
   c) 65 miles per hour

579. A **gallon** equals four _____.
   a) quarters
   b) cups
   c) quarts

580. A **hole in one** is good in _____.
   a) golf
   b) boxing
   c) basketball

581. A **yard** is a little less than a _____.
   a) mile
   b) foot
   c) meter

582. **Salespeople** at department stores sell _____.
   a) apartments
   b) clothing and appliances
   c) fresh fruit and vegetables

583. People _____.
   a) **play** frisbee
   b) **drink** frisbee
   c) **eat** frisbee

584. A man named George received a **Dear John** letter. He probably _____.
   a) has lost his girlfriend
   b) has a new address
   c) has changed his name

Phrases and Idioms

PART TWO

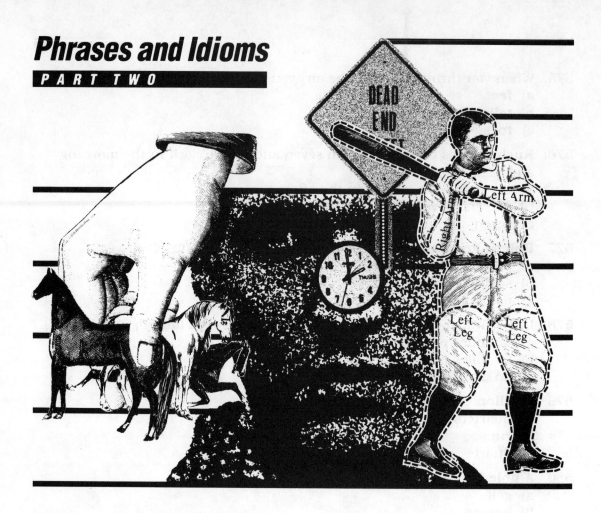

Directions: Complete the sentences.

585. If **it's up to you**, it's _____.
    a) your decision
    b) your height
    c) your idea

586. When people say, "**Drop me a line**," they want you to _____.
    a) go fishing with them
    b) write to them
    c) forget about them

587. **Keep your shirt on** means _____.
    a) be patient
    b) don't undress
    c) dress well

588. A **dead end street** is one that _____.
    a) is dangerous
    b) has a cemetery on it
    c) has no exit

589. **Fast food** restaurants have food that _____.
    a) is cooked and served quickly
    b) is cooked at your table
    c) is cooked without any oil

590. A **home run** is good in _____.
    a) a computer program
    b) a football game
    c) a baseball game

591. When a person asks, "**Do you need a lift**?", she wants to know if you need _____.
    a) an elevator
    b) a ride in her car
    c) shoes with high heels

592. Your mother's **maiden name** is _____.
    a) her nickname
    b) her maid's name
    c) her family name before she got married

593. I'd like to **sleep on it** means I'd like to _____.
    a) put it under my pillow
    b) hide it in my bed
    c) take more time to decide

594. A **private eye** is a _____.
    a) detective
    b) pair of glasses
    c) diary

595. They **hit it off** means they _____.
    a) got into a fight
    b) played ball
    c) got along well

596. Scotch **on the rocks** is a drink _____.
    a) with loud music
    b) with ice cubes
    c) you take to the mountains

597. A person who can **carry a tune** _____.
    a) sings well
    b) is strong
    c) has a songbook

598. Joe said he was forty years old when he was really fifty years old. He told a _____.
    a) **black lie**
    b) **white lie**
    c) **red lie**

599. When you **grab a bite**, you _____.
    a) eat a meal quickly
    b) bite someone
    c) take someone's food

600. This season hats are **in** means hats are now _____.
    a) worn inside
    b) expensive
    c) in fashion

601. When you **give up**, you _____.
    a) start flying
    b) try buying
    c) stop trying

602. A person with a **sweet tooth** _____.
    a) likes candy
    b) has false teeth
    c) has only one tooth

603. I can do it **in no time** means _____.
    a) I can never do it
    b) I can do it quickly
    c) It will take a long time to do

604. She doesn't have a husband. She's _____.
    a) **bringing in** her children alone
    b) **bringing out** her children alone
    c) **bringing up** her children alone

605. I'm **fed up** means I'm _____.
    a) not hungry
    b) angry
    c) afraid

606. An **absent-minded professor** is a _____.
    a) forgetful person
    b) funny person
    c) foolish teacher

607. Someone who **got caught in a shower** was _____.
    a) found in the bathroom
    b) outside when it began to rain
    c) at a party

608. He talks a lot but says nothing. He talks _____.
    a) **in rhymes**
    b) **in squares**
    c) **in circles**

609. When Mrs. Barton talks about her **late** husband, she means her husband _____.
a) never comes early
b) always keeps her waiting
c) is dead

610. A **well-to-do** person is _____.
a) healthy
b) rich
c) heavy

611. You can **steal a base** in _____.
a) the army
b) a basement
c) baseball

612. Someone with a problem doesn't say, "I'm _____."
a) **in a jam**
b) **in a tomato**
c) **in a pickle**

613. To **take a stand** is _____.
a) to stand up
b) to climb a stepladder
c) to express a strong opinion

614. A person who can't **make a living**, can't _____.
a) earn enough money to live on
b) make friends
c) find someone to live with

615. We say "**Get to the point**" when someone is _____.
a) sharpening a pencil
b) climbing a mountain
c) not saying what he means

616. If you have **butterflies in your stomach**, you feel _____.
a) nervous
b) full
c) angry

617. When a recipe in a cookbook says to **separate two eggs**, you _____.
a) put each egg in a different place
b) make sure the eggs don't touch
c) separate the white from the yolk

618. You get a **tune up** for your _____.
a) car
b) body
c) piano

619. **Sold out** means _____.
    a) you pay outside
    b) there aren't any left
    c) you are at an outdoor market

620. When the rain **lets up**, it _____.
    a) slows down
    b) starts again
    c) changes direction

621. If your friend says, "**Keep in touch**," he _____.
    a) wants to hold your hand
    b) wants you to write
    c) wants you to stay nearby

622. People use a **second coat** when they _____.
    a) want to steal
    b) catch a cold
    c) paint a room

623. A **night owl** _____.
    a) sleeps well at night
    b) sees well at night
    c) stays up at night

624. A **sore loser** is a person who _____.
    a) was hurt but got better
    b) is angry that he didn't win
    c) lost money in a fight

625. A **social butterfly** enjoys _____.
    a) flying a kite
    b) going to parties
    c) changing clothes

626. A person with **two left feet** can't _____.
    a) dance
    b) walk
    c) drive

627. A friend says she is **free** at three. She means _____.
    a) she is getting a divorce at three o'clock
    b) she is leaving jail at three o'clock
    c) she is not busy at three o'clock

628. I'm **counting on** you means I'm _____.
    a) giving you money
    b) taking your number
    c) depending on you

629. You're **on the right track** means you're _____.
a) going uptown
b) doing something right
c) traveling by train

630. Something **on sale** is _____.
a) cheaper than before
b) ready for a boat trip
c) more expensive than before

631. She **made up her mind** means she _____.
a) made a decision
b) put on make-up
c) put on a hat

632. At the end of a business letter, you may write, "_____."
a) **Sincerely,**
b) **Fondly,**
c) **Your friend,**

633. If a man says, "This steak is **too well done**," he means _____.
a) the steak is just right
b) the steak was cooked too long
c) the steak wasn't cooked enough

634. When the score is **six-all**, _____.
a) both teams have six points
b) one team is ahead by six points
c) one team needs six more points to win

635. A **teacher's pet** is his _____.
a) French poodle
b) Siamese cat
c) favorite student

636. Someone says, "**Man on first**. **One out**." He is talking about _____.
a) elevators
b) a baseball game
c) a soccer game

637. A **light sleeper** _____.
a) wakes up easily
b) doesn't use blankets
c) isn't very heavy

638. When you don't want to answer a question, a polite response
is "_____."
a) **None of your business**
b) **Mind your own business**
c) **I'd rather not say**

639. You are in a restaurant and you want the bill. You say, "_____."
    a) **Check, please**
    b) **Check, here**
    c) **Please, check**

640. You are in a restaurant. You don't know where the bathroom is. You ask, "_____?"
    a) **Where's the washing room**
    b) **Where's the bathroom**
    c) **Where's the rest room**

641. A friend enters a contest. You say, "_____!"
    a) **Good luck**
    b) **Best wishes**
    c) **Congratulations**

642. Something unexpected is _____.
    a) **out of the gold**
    b) **out of the black**
    c) **out of the blue**

643. If someone says, "You're wearing a beautiful belt," you say, "_____."
    a) **Never mind**
    b) **Thanks**
    c) **Yes, I know**

644. You want someone to do something for you. You say, "_____?"
    a) **Would you do me a favor**
    b) **Would you favor me**
    c) **Do you favor me**

645. We don't eat _____.
    a) **an ear of corn**
    b) **a head of lettuce**
    c) **the eye of a potato**

646. When you **get up on the wrong side of the bed**, you are _____.
    a) sleepy
    b) in a bad mood
    c) confused

647. When you step on someone's toe, you say, "_____."
    a) **It was your fault**
    b) **I'm sorry**
    c) **My mistake**

648. A **down-to-earth** person is _____.
    a) short
    b) poor
    c) natural

649. Someone says, "**I'd like to make a toast**." He is going to _____.
    a) prepare a big breakfast
    b) bake a loaf of bread
    c) drink to someone's health

650. Two o'clock **on the nose** is _____.
    a) exactly two o'clock
    b) a little before two o'clock
    c) a little after two o'clock

651. When you're at the dinner table and you want the salt,
    you say, "_____."
    a) **Please pass the salt**
    b) **Hand over the salt**
    c) **Salt my food, please**

652. If spring is **just around the corner**, it _____.
    a) is almost here
    b) has almost ended
    c) keeps coming and going

653. When you want to smoke, you should ask, "_____?"
    a) **Would I please be able to smoke**
    b) **Do you mind if I smoke**
    c) **Shall I smoke**

654. Your friend asks, "Would you like **seconds**?" She is asking if you want
    more _____.
    a) food
    b) time
    c) room

655. When a friend wants you to be more patient, she might say, "_____!"
    a) **Hold your horses**
    b) **Play possum**
    c) **Clam up**

656. A **blind date** is a date with someone _____.
    a) who hasn't met you before
    b) who cannot see
    c) who is not good-looking

657. A **soap opera** is _____.
    a) classical music
    b) music for a bath
    c) a TV love story

658. You say **knock on wood** when you _____.
    a) visit a friend at her home
    b) want a good thing to continue
    c) see a woodpecker

659. When someone tells you to use **elbow grease**, you _____.
   a) see a doctor
   b) go to the supermarket
   c) work harder

660. When you get **cold cuts**, you _____.
   a) heat them
   b) eat them
   c) bandage them

661. When someone says, "**No wonder** she's tired," he is _____.
   a) surprised she's tired
   b) not surprised she's tired
   c) sorry that she's tired

662. What comes **hot off the press**? _____.
   a) pancakes
   b) pants
   c) newspapers

663. When you put plates, knives, forks, spoons and napkins on the table, you _____.
   a) **cover the table**
   b) **set the table**
   c) **fix the table**

664. An area in which you can't smoke has a _____.
   a) **Don't smoke** sign
   b) **No smoking** sign
   c) **Not to smoke** sign

665. When you go on **a wild goose chase**, you _____.
   a) don't accomplish anything
   b) hunt wild animals
   c) get a lot of exercise

666. A doctor might ask a patient, "_____?"
   a) **What's the matter**
   b) **What's up**
   c) **What possesses you**

667. A man who was **let go** needs a new _____.
   a) job
   b) wife
   c) belt

668. "**What a wise guy!**" is a phrase for _____.
   a) an intelligent person
   b) a dishonest person
   c) a know-it-all

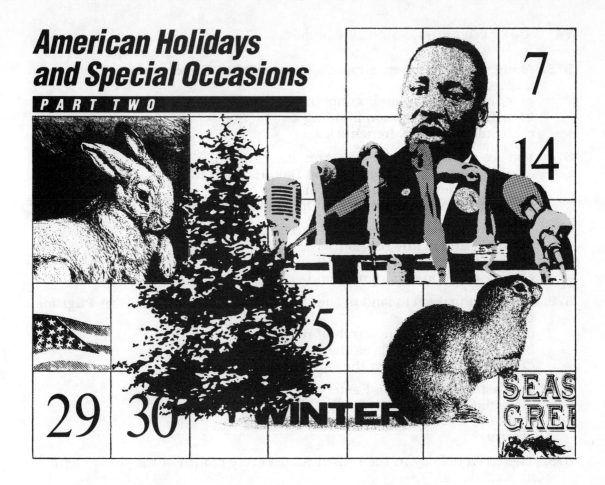

American Holidays and Special Occasions

PART TWO

Directions: Complete the sentences.

669. For **Halloween**, people carve faces on _____.
  a) trees
  b) apples
  c) pumpkins

670. A **New Year's resolution** is a _____.
  a) sugar-free diet
  b) wish for the New Year
  c) decision to do something new

671. **Martin Luther King Day** honors the man who fought prejudice with _____.
  a) terrorism
  b) non-violence
  c) money

672. Many people wear green on _____.
  a) **Christmas Day**
  b) **St. Patrick's Day**
  c) **Labor Day**

673. Along with the turkey, a typical **Thanksgiving dinner** includes
_____.

  a) cranberry sauce and pumpkin pie
  b) baked ham and plum pudding
  c) hamburgers and french fries

674. You see more **flags** than usual on _____.
  a) New Year's Day, Thanksgiving Day, Halloween
  b) July 4, Memorial Day, Veteran's Day
  c) Valentine's Day, April Fool's Day, Easter

675. You send a **Season's Greetings** card _____.
  a) to a friend of any religion
  b) only to a Christian friend
  c) only to a non-Christian friend

676. The first Puritans to land in the United States called themselves **Pilgrims**
because _____.
  a) they traveled far in search of religious freedom
  b) they took many pills as they traveled
  c) they were grim when they arrived

677. An **Easter bonnet** is an Easter _____.
  a) rabbit
  b) hat
  c) seal

678. There is a holiday in the United States every month of the year except
_____.
  a) **September**
  b) **March**
  c) **August**

679. On the night of **July 4**, there are many _____.
  a) parades
  b) costume parties
  c) firework displays

680. **McDonald's** and **Burger King** are places where some Americans
have _____.
  a) their weddings
  b) their anniversary parties
  c) their children's birthday parties

681. **To vote** in the United States, a person must be a U.S. citizen. That person
must also be at least eighteen years old and _____.
  a) register to vote
  b) have a bank account
  c) have a high school diploma

682. A **housewarming party** is a party _____.
  a) in a cold house
  b) in a new house
  c) in a hot house

683. When we speak of **Christmas** or **New Year's Eve**, we mean _____.
    a) the week of the holiday
    b) the day after the holiday
    c) the night before the holiday

684. On **Washington's Birthday**, **Lincoln's Birthday** and **Columbus Day** there are always big _____.
    a) firework displays
    b) sales in the stores
    c) campfires

685. People play tricks on their friends on _____.
    a) **April 1**
    b) **May 1**
    c) **June 1**

686. Your friend has just become **engaged**. You say, "_____."
    a) I wish you a speedy recovery
    b) I'm so happy for you
    c) Better luck next time

687. **Parking rules** on holidays are often the same as parking rules on _____.
    a) Sunday
    b) Saturday
    c) Friday

688. There is a story that as a child **George Washington** chopped down his father's favorite _____.
    a) apple tree
    b) pear tree
    c) cherry tree

689. On **Graduation Day** graduates receive _____.
    a) big bills
    b) diplomas
    c) receipts

690. People often have picnics and barbeques on _____.
    a) **Veteran's Day and Columbus Day**
    b) **Valentine's Day and Easter**
    c) **July 4 and Labor Day**

691. **Christopher Columbus** was able to sail to America because of the help of _____.
    a) King George III of England
    b) Queen Isabella of Spain
    c) King John II of Portugal

692. **Columbus Day**, **Washington's Birthday** and **Lincoln's Birthday** are no longer celebrated on the day of the holiday, but on the closest _____.
    a) Monday
    b) Friday
    c) Sunday

693. The start of spring is the best time for _____.
    a) doing **spring cleaning**
    b) eating **spring chicken**
    c) drinking **spring water**

694. **George Washington** is sometimes called "_____."
    a) the Grandfather of our Country
    b) the Father of our Country
    c) the Godfather of our Country

695. A **gold watch** used to be a common gift when a person _____.
    a) got fired
    b) retired
    c) expired

696. When you join a **Christmas Club** at a bank, you _____.
    a) save money every week until Christmas
    b) sing Christmas songs for poor people
    c) give money to poor people

697. Sometimes for **Easter**, children enjoy egg-rolling contests. The most famous egg-rolling contest in the United States takes place _____.
    a) on the White House lawn
    b) at Disney World
    c) at St. Patrick's Cathedral

698. Which holiday is a day for family reunions? _____.
    a) **April Fool's Day**
    b) **Columbus Day**
    c) **Thanksgiving Day**

699. The main streets of most American cities are gaily decorated _____.
    a) during the **summer** season
    b) during the **spring** season
    c) during the **Christmas** season

700. **"Jingle Bells"** _____.
    a) is a Christmas song
    b) are Christmas decorations
    c) are the bells that ring in the New Year

701. A green stripe used to be painted on Fifth Avenue in New York City for the _____.
    a) **Thanksgiving Day** parade
    b) **Columbus Day** parade
    c) **St. Patrick's Day** parade

702. For most Americans the weekends of **Memorial Day** and **Labor Day** are for _____.
    a) fun
    b) prayer
    c) study

703. On **Sadie Hawkins Day** women chase men. If a woman catches a man, he must _____.
     a) kiss her
     b) pay her
     c) marry her

704. If a groundhog sees his shadow on **Groundhog Day**, _____.
     a) spring will be here soon
     b) there will be six more weeks of winter
     c) there will be a snowstorm the next week

705. One of the most popular Christmas plants is the **holly**. This plant has _____.
     a) pointed leaves and red berries
     b) silver leaves and pink flowers
     c) white and yellow flowers

706. When the Pilgrims came to America, they landed at _____.
     a) **Eden Rock**
     b) **Plymouth Rock**
     c) **Rockefeller Plaza**

707. During the **Christmas season**, some people decorate their _____.
     a) cars and bicycles
     b) backyards and basements
     c) windows and front lawns

708. **Thanksgiving** is a _____.
     a) boat festival
     b) harvest festival
     c) moon festival

709. When do you send a **sympathy card**? When _____.
     a) you want to let your friend know how much you like him
     b) a person has gone to the hospital
     c) a friend or relative has died

710. **June** is the month of _____.
     a) brides
     b) babies
     c) grandmothers

711. At a **funeral** people usually wear _____.
     a) white clothes
     b) red clothes
     c) black clothes

712. At a **wedding** the unmarried women stand in line and try to catch _____.
     a) the bride's shoe
     b) the bride's bouquet
     c) the bride's veil

713. A **bachelor party** is given shortly before a man _____.
     a) gets married
     b) leaves the army
     c) graduates from college

714. On **Primary Day** _____.
     a) the year begins
     b) children start school
     c) some people vote

715. Before the **wedding ceremony**, it is a tradition for the bride not to
     see _____.
     a) her mother
     b) her father
     c) her husband-to-be

716. Some people put popcorn on a string and use it as decoration
     for their _____.
     a) **Halloween costume**
     b) **Christmas tree**
     c) **Easter basket**

717. What holiday honors the working man? _____.
     a) **Halloween**
     b) **Veteran's Day**
     c) **Labor Day**

718. On **Memorial Day** we decorate the graves of the dead with flowers.
     Memorial Day used to be called _____.
     a) Day of the Dead
     b) Decoration Day
     c) Flower Day

719. People put balls, lights and tinsel _____.
     a) on **Christmas trees**
     b) in **Easter baskets**
     c) in **pumpkins**

720. We **turn over a new leaf** on _____.
     a) April 1
     b) April 15
     c) January 1

721. Some children collect money on **Halloween** and give it to _____.
     a) their grandparents
     b) their sisters and brothers
     c) UNICEF

722. On what holiday does a friend say "There is a green spot on your nose"
     when there isn't any spot on your nose? _____.
     a) **April Fool's Day**
     b) **St. Patrick's Day**
     c) **Halloween**

723. **On holidays**, buses and trains run _____.
   a) more often than usual
   b) less often than usual
   c) the same as usual

724. You receive a **birth announcement** when _____.
   a) you are a baby
   b) you have just had a baby
   c) you know someone who has had a baby

725. Every four years on **January 20** _____.
   a) the president begins his winter vacation
   b) the new president is sworn into office
   c) the president speaks at the United Nations

726. At **Christmas time** many companies give their employees Christmas
   _____.
   a) bonuses
   b) stockings
   c) bells

727. People hang stockings which will be filled with small gifts on _____.
   a) **New Year's Eve**
   b) **Christmas Eve**
   c) **Valentine's Day**

728. The **groundhog** comes out of his hole and looks for his shadow on the
   second day of _____.
   a) January
   b) February
   c) March

729. At Christmas time people often hang a branch of **mistletoe**. When they
   walk under it, they _____.
   a) shake hands
   b) drink
   c) kiss

730. What do children say on **Halloween**? _____.
   a) Dance to the beat
   b) Let me eat
   c) Trick or treat

731. Before an **election** the candidates spend a lot of money
   on their _____.
   a) wives or husbands
   b) campaign
   c) party

732. A **farewell party** is for someone who is going _____.
   a) to heaven
   b) to a hospital
   c) away

733. **Mardi Gras** is a six day celebration with parades and costume balls. The most famous Mardi Gras celebration in the United States takes place in _____.
    a) New Orleans
    b) Miami
    c) Atlanta

734. When **Christopher Columbus** arrived in the New World, he thought _____.
    a) he had discovered a new world
    b) he had discovered a short route to India
    c) he had discovered the world was flat

735. The **bridesmaids** at a wedding usually _____.
    a) receive money
    b) take part in the wedding ceremony
    c) clean up after the wedding

736. At a wedding the **father of the bride** is supposed to _____.
    a) pay the bride
    b) give the bride away
    c) kiss the bride's hand

737. When you are at a **prom**, you are at _____.
    a) a wedding
    b) a school dance
    c) a picnic

738. When you are invited to an **Open House** from one o'clock to five o'clock, you _____.
    a) should arrive at exactly one o'clock
    b) may come any time between one o'clock and five o'clock
    c) should arrive shortly after one o'clock

739. During a **leap year** we _____.
    a) jump high
    b) add a day
    c) skip a month

740. When a friend sends you an invitation which has **RSVP** on it, _____.
    a) you should let your friend know if you can go
    b) you don't have to respond to the invitation
    c) you only have to reply if you can't go

741. At **campfires** children enjoy listening to _____.
    a) fairy tales
    b) ghost stories
    c) nursery rhymes

742. People stand with a drink in their hand and talk to many different guests at a _____.
    a) **birthday party**
    b) **dinner party**
    c) **cocktail party**

743. At a **traditional wedding**, the bride wears "something old, something new, something borrowed, and something _____."
   a) in her shoe
   b) made with glue
   c) blue

744. When a **new ship** goes on its first trip, a famous person _____.
   a) breaks a bottle of champagne on it
   b) kisses the captain of the ship
   c) throws a bucket of water on it

745. Children **bob for apples** when they are at a _____.
   a) beach party
   b) Halloween party
   c) Christmas party

746. In California on New Year's day, there is a big parade of roses followed by an important football game. This event is called the _____.
   a) **Rose Bowl**
   b) **Rose Ball**
   c) **Rose Bush**

747. **Commencement Exercises** take place _____.
   a) at a new job
   b) at a graduation
   c) before a sports event

748. A **party favor** is a small _____.
   a) gift you bring to a party
   b) gift you receive at a party
   c) job you do to help clean up after a party

749. On **Election Day** people go to the _____.
   a) polls
   b) post office
   c) bank

750. At **ticker tape parades** for returning heros, people throw _____.
   a) candy
   b) rice
   c) paper

751. The day graduates return to their high schools and colleges for a big football game, parties and festivities is called _____.
   a) **Orientation**
   b) **Homecoming**
   c) **Finals**

752. At a **buffet supper**, you _____.
   a) bring a bouquet
   b) wear your best clothes
   c) serve yourself

Vocabulary
PART TWO

Directions: Complete the sentences.

753. A **highchair** is a chair for a _____.
    a) king
    b) giant
    c) baby

754. A **pharmacist** _____.
    a) works on a farm
    b) prepares medicine
    c) takes care of animals

755. When people say "**Got it**?", they mean "Do you _____?"
    a) like it
    b) understand
    c) dislike it

756. People send friends who are sick _____.
   a) **friendship cards**
   b) **condolence cards**
   c) **get well cards**

757. When you are not sure of something, you shouldn't begin "_____."
   a) **In my opinion**
   b) **I think**
   c) **The fact is**

758. When you have a problem, you _____.
   a) **ask** a friend to help you
   b) **tell** a friend to help you
   c) **advise** a friend to help you

759. When a woman gives birth to two children on the same day, the children are called _____.
   a) **pairs**
   b) **doubles**
   c) **twins**

760. People eat ice cream, cake or cookies for _____.
   a) **dessert**
   b) **an appetizer**
   c) **dinner**

761. If you think fifteen dollars is very little to pay for a shirt, you say, "_____."
   a) It's **only** fifteen dollars
   b) It's **about** fifteen dollars
   c) It's **exactly** fifteen dollars

762. When you arrive late at a sports event and want to know what's happening, you ask, "_____?"
   a) **Who has an advantage**
   b) **What are the points**
   c) **What's the score**

763. When you want to be sure nobody can open a door, you _____.
   a) **slam** it
   b) **lock** it
   c) **shut** it

764. When people stay in the sun for a long time, they get a _____.
   a) **sunset**
   b) **sunburn**
   c) **sundae**

765. A man who wants a **snapshot** of his wife, needs a _____.
   a) gun
   b) camera
   c) paintbrush

766. When people enjoy a performance and want more, they call out "_____!"
  a) **Repeat**
  b) **Again**
  c) **Encore**

767. When you live in an apartment that you don't own, you pay the landlord _____.
  a) **rent**
  b) **tuition**
  c) **admission**

768. When you cut your finger, you cover the cut with a _____.
  a) **Band-Aid**
  b) **bandit**
  c) **bandana**

769. When you are enjoying yourself, you are _____.
  a) **funny**
  b) **having fun**
  c) **fundamental**

770. Matching jackets and pants are called _____.
  a) **costumes**
  b) **suites**
  c) **suits**

771. It isn't raining hard. It's just _____.
  a) **dazzling**
  b) **sizzling**
  c) **drizzling**

772. A ceremony for the dead is called a _____.
  a) **parade**
  b) **funeral**
  c) **wedding**

773. A person's **step-father** is his _____.
  a) mother's husband but not his father
  b) wife's father
  c) mother's brother

774. The leader of an orchestra is the _____.
  a) **ruler**
  b) **general**
  c) **conductor**

775. When you travel on a bus, a taxi, a train or a plane, you have to pay _____.
  a) **tuition**
  b) the **fare**
  c) a **tax**

776. When you want to see a doctor, you make _____.
    a) **an appointment**
    b) **a fuss**
    c) **a rendezvous**

777. When the score is the same for two teams, the score is _____.
    a) **equalled**
    b) **doubled**
    c) **tied**

778. Last week I _____.
    a) **met** a beautiful painting
    b) **saw** a beautiful painting
    c) **knew** a beautiful painting

779. When a married couple legally ends their marriage, they get _____.
    a) **divorced**
    b) **diplomas**
    c) **engaged**

780. The room directly under the roof of a house is the _____.
    a) **basement**
    b) **cellar**
    c) **attic**

781. A **typical** day is a _____.
    a) usual day
    b) hot and humid day
    c) strange day

782. A woman **polishes** her shoes and her _____.
    a) face
    b) nose
    c) nails

783. A person who looks **ill** needs _____.
    a) eyeglasses
    b) a doctor
    c) a hairdresser

784. A **pill** is _____.
    a) medicine in a tablet
    b) money you owe
    c) a loud bell

785. A person between the ages of thirteen and nineteen is a _____.
    a) **delinquent**
    b) **teenager**
    c) **toddler**

786. At a private school, you pay _____.
  a) **rent**
  b) **a toll**
  c) **tuition**

787. If Alex Weiss **was fired** last night, today he _____.
  a) is dead
  b) has a burn
  c) is unemployed

788. A play, movie or book is called a **hit** when it is _____.
  a) successful
  b) unsuccessful
  c) violent

789. People don't like _____.
  a) **roaches** in their home
  b) **riches** in their home
  c) **rugs** in their home

790. When you need money, you go to the bank and ask for a _____.
  a) **loan**
  b) **gift**
  c) **bill**

791. A housewife is the same as a _____.
  a) **caretaker**
  b) **maid**
  c) **homemaker**

792. A man who pulls rabbits out of a hat is a _____.
  a) **musician**
  b) **physician**
  c) **magician**

793. A **lollipop** is a _____.
  a) nickname for a father
  b) candy on a stick
  c) song to put a child to sleep

794. When you **dust** furniture, you _____.
  a) clean it
  b) make it dirty
  c) put powder on it

795. A person between the ages of forty and sixty-five is _____.
  a) **ripe**
  b) **elderly**
  c) **middle-aged**

796. Before you go to a restaurant, you should call and make a _____.
    a) **date**
    b) **reservation**
    c) **plan**

797. **In-laws** are _____.
    a) criminals
    b) lawyers
    c) relatives by marriage

798. A person who is careful with money is _____.
    a) **economic**
    b) **economical**
    c) **rich**

799. The **eighteenth century** goes from _____.
    a) 1700-1800
    b) 1800-1900
    c) 1600-1700

800. When you **go to the country**, you _____.
    a) go to your native land
    b) leave the city
    c) go to the capital

801. When a man removes the hair from his face with a razor, he is _____.
    a) **shaving**
    b) **mowing**
    c) **cutting**

802. The opposite of **division** is _____.
    a) **addition**
    b) **subtraction**
    c) **multiplication**

803. The opposite of a **crooked** line is a _____.
    a) **fine** line
    b) **straight** line
    c) **double** line

804. A long, wide main road is a _____.
    a) **highway**
    b) **driveway**
    c) **path**

805. Shoes that are too big or too small don't _____.
    a) **fit**
    b) **wear**
    c) **work**

806. A **busybody** is a _____.
    a) hard worker
    b) noisy person
    c) nosy person

807. Valuable old objects are called _____.
    a) **junk**
    b) **elders**
    c) **antiques**

808. When you want your roast beef pink and juicy, you order it _____.
    a) **raw**
    b) **rare**
    c) **bloody**

809. You usually wear a belt around your _____.
    a) **ankle**
    b) **waist**
    c) **wrist**

810. We call a person **strange** if he is _____.
    a) odd
    b) unfriendly
    c) foreign

811. When you don't pronounce words the way a native speaker does, you have _____.
    a) a **misprint**
    b) an **accent**
    c) an **error**

812. When something isn't important, it doesn't _____.
    a) **mind**
    b) **matter**
    c) **work**

813. The opposite of **war** is _____.
    a) **quiet**
    b) **light**
    c) **peace**

814. The hair on an animal is called its _____.
    a) **tail**
    b) **fur**
    c) **beard**

815. The opposite of **even** is _____.
    a) **odd**
    b) **strange**
    c) **equal**

816. Two lines that go in the same direction but do not touch are _____.
     a) **parallel**
     b) **perpendicular**
     c) **unequal**

817. The opposite of **dangerous** is _____.
     a) **exciting**
     b) **safe**
     c) **difficult**

818. People without hair on their head are _____.
     a) **clean**
     b) **bold**
     c) **bald**

819. Parents push their babies in _____.
     a) **carts**
     b) **boxes**
     c) **strollers**

820. A person who takes things from your pocket is a _____.
     a) **tailor**
     b) **mugger**
     c) **pickpocket**

821. 212 degrees Fahrenheit is the _____.
     a) **freezing point** of water
     b) **boiling point** of water
     c) **melting point** of water

822. When invited to someone's home, you are a _____.
     a) **guest**
     b) **ghost**
     c) **host**

823. When you don't have enough money to pay for a car, you can't _____.
     a) **add** it
     b) **accept** it
     c) **afford** it

824. You sew with a needle and _____.
     a) **thread**
     b) **wool**
     c) **string**

825. A body of land surrounded by water is called _____.
     a) a **mountain**
     b) an **island**
     c) a **castle**

826. The dividing line between two countries is called the _____.
    a) **edge**
    b) **limit**
    c) **border**

827. You **shiver** when you are _____.
    a) hot
    b) sad
    c) cold

828. The opposite of **clever** is _____.
    a) **stupid**
    b) **lazy**
    c) **happy**

829. A person who can fix things is _____.
    a) **handsome**
    b) **handy**
    c) **artistic**

830. You cover yourself with a _____.
    a) **blanket**
    b) **mattress**
    c) **pillow**

831. When you want to know how to get somewhere, you ask for _____.
    a) **directions**
    b) **details**
    c) **sections**

832. A doctor who performs operations is a _____.
    a) **sergeant**
    b) **serpent**
    c) **surgeon**

833. At a restaurant, if you want fish that was never frozen, you ask for _____.
    a) **new** fish
    b) **hot** fish
    c) **fresh** fish

834. Many people in cities live in _____.
    a) **departments**
    b) **apartments**
    c) **cabins**

835. Someone you pay to watch your children is called a _____.
    a) **babysitter**
    b) **watchguard**
    c) **social worker**

American History, Geography and Government

PART TWO

Directions: Change the sentences.

836. The **president's cabinet** refers to _____.
    a) furniture in the White House
    b) advisers elected to help the president
    c) advisers chosen by the president

837. The three states that border on the Pacific Ocean are California, Oregon and _____.
    a) **Nebraska**
    b) **New Mexico**
    c) **Washington**

838. The United States government has a system of **checks and balances**. This _____.
    a) balances the power of the branches of government
    b) balances business and government
    c) balances church and state

839. When the United States became an independent nation, there were
_____.

   a) **three colonies**
   b) **thirteen colonies**
   c) **thirty colonies**

840. The **distance from Canada to Mexico** is about _____.
   a) 500 miles
   b) 3000 miles
   c) 1400 miles

841. What is the **official religion** of the United States? _____.
   a) Christianity
   b) There is no official religion
   c) Christianity and Judaism

842. It was illegal to drink or sell alcohol during the time called _____.
   a) **Prohibition**
   b) **the Depression**
   c) **the New Deal**

843. The **Nineteenth Amendment** to the Constitution became a law in 1920.
It gave women the right to _____.
   a) vote
   b) smoke
   c) work

844. There are four branches of **the Armed Forces**. They are the Army, the Navy,
the Air Force and the _____.
   a) Police
   b) Marines
   c) National Guard

845. The **highest building** in the United States is the _____.
   a) World Trade Center in New York City
   b) Sears Tower in Chicago
   c) Fairmont Hotel in San Francisco

846. **Betsy Ross** _____.
   a) made the first American flag
   b) helped free many slaves
   c) was married to an American president

847. The **Declaration of Independence** was written by _____.
   a) Abraham Lincoln
   b) George Washington
   c) Thomas Jefferson

848. Most **American Indians** live in _____.
   a) Maine
   b) Arizona
   c) California

849. What structure stands in New York harbor and welcomes immigrants to the United States? _____.
    a) **The World Trade Center**
    b) **The Empire State Building**
    c) **The Statue of Liberty**

850. The symbol of the **Democratic Party** is _____.
    a) an elephant
    b) a rabbit
    c) a donkey

851. The **D.C.** in Washington, D.C. stands for _____.
    a) Door to the Capital
    b) Democratic Center
    c) District of Columbia

852. Which state has more people than any other state? _____.
    a) **Florida**
    b) **Texas**
    c) **California**

853. Which famous patriot said, "Give me liberty, or give me death?" _____.
    a) **Patrick Henry**
    b) **John F. Kennedy**
    c) **Richard Nixon**

854. From coast to coast, the **continental United States** covers about _____.
    a) 2000 miles
    b) 3000 miles
    c) 1500 miles

855. Which state has a **semi-tropical climate**? _____.
    a) Virginia
    b) South Carolina
    c) Florida

856. Who is the **commander-in-chief** of the United States Armed Forces? _____.
    a) The president of the United States
    b) The secretary of defense
    c) The top ranking five star general

857. Many **Mormons** live in _____.
    a) California
    b) Utah
    c) Nevada

858. What was founded in San Francisco in 1945? _____.
    a) **The World Court**
    b) **The League of Nations**
    c) **The United Nations**

859. The elephant is the symbol of the _____.
   a) **Democratic Party**
   b) **Republican Party**
   c) **Conservative Party**

860. During the **Boston Tea Party** _____.
   a) British soldiers invited soldiers from Boston to drink tea
   b) the British king gave a party for the people of Boston
   c) people from Boston threw British tea into Boston harbor

861. The **federal government** is _____.
   a) the national government
   b) the state government
   c) the local (city) government

862. Which United States president left office as a result of the
   Watergate Scandal? _____.
   a) Lyndon Johnson
   b) Richard M. Nixon
   c) Gerald Ford

863. The **United States Congress** has two parts, the Senate and the _____.
   a) Supreme Court
   b) Executive Branch
   c) House of Representatives

864. The **largest city in the Midwest** of the United States is _____.
   a) Chicago, Illinois
   b) Madison, Wisconsin
   c) Detroit, Michigan

865. The heads of four United States presidents are carved in a mountain in
   South Dakota. The mountain is called _____.
   a) **Mount Vernon**
   b) **Mount Rushmore**
   c) **Mount Washington**

866. **Dixie** is another name for _____.
   a) the South
   b) the Northeast
   c) the West

867. How many **judges** are there on the United States Supreme Court?
   _____.
   a) fifteen
   b) nine
   c) three

868. The **Declaration of Independence** states that people have the right to seek
   _____.
   a) love
   b) marriage
   c) happiness

HOMES

869. There are **five Great Lakes** between the United States and Canada.
Two of the Great Lakes are _____.
a) Lake Michigan and Lake Ontario
b) Lake Madison and Lake Ohio
c) Lake Maryland and Lake Oregon

870. When **people vote** for the president of the United States,
they _____.
a) vote directly for the president
b) vote for electors who vote for the president
c) vote for a party and not a person

871. **Presidential advisers** keep their jobs for as long as _____.
a) they like
b) the president likes
c) the voters like

872. **Abraham Lincoln** _____.
a) was against slavery
b) was for slavery
c) was a slave

873. The region which includes Connecticut, Rhode Island, Massachusetts,
Vermont, New Hampshire and Maine is called _____.
a) **New Amsterdam**
b) **New America**
c) **New England**

874. What city in Louisiana was settled by the French? _____.
a) **New Orleans**
b) **Atlanta**
c) **Tampa**

875. Only two men were president of the United States in the 18th century.
One of them was **George Washington**; the other was _____.
a) **John Smith**
b) **James Madison**
c) **John Adams**

876. The first man to sign the Declaration of Independence was **John Hancock**.
Today a person's John Hancock is his _____.
a) independence
b) signature
c) name

877. The **capital of New York State** is _____.
a) New York City
b) Buffalo
c) Albany

878. Which state borders on the **Gulf of Mexico**? _____.
a) New Mexico
b) Texas
c) Arizona

879. **The Declaration of Independence** was written in the year _____.
    a) 1776
    b) 1861
    c) 1607

880. **The Gettysburg Address** is one of the shortest and most famous speeches in American history. This speech was written by _____.
    a) John F. Kennedy
    b) Thomas Jefferson
    c) Abraham Lincoln

881. "Ask not what your country can do for you, but what you can do for your country." These are the words of _____.
    a) **Franklin D. Roosevelt**
    b) **John F. Kennedy**
    c) **Thomas Jefferson**

882. United States **senators** are elected for _____.
    a) two years
    b) four years
    c) six years

883. **Ponce de Leon** thought he had found the fountain of youth when he visited what is now the state of _____.
    a) New Mexico
    b) Florida
    c) Louisiana

884. The men who serve on **the Supreme Court** are called _____.
    a) justices
    b) lords
    c) liberals

885. In 1776 Thomas Paine wrote a short booklet called **Common Sense**. In it he told Americans to form a new government without _____.
    a) taxes
    b) an army
    c) a king

886. This famous American was a writer, a scientist, an inventor and a diplomat. He started the first public library and the first fire department. He was _____.
    a) **Benjamin Franklin**
    b) **Thomas Edison**
    c) **George Washington**

887. At **Williamsburg, Virginia** you can see how Americans lived in _____.
    a) Ancient times
    b) Colonial times
    c) Frontier times

888. Today Texas is in the area of the United States called the _____.
    a) **Wild West**
    b) **Sun Belt**
    c) **New Frontier**

889. The **Amish** are religious people who lead a simple life without electricity, cars, or TV. Most Amish live in _____.
    a) Lancaster, Pennsylvania
    b) Brooklyn, New York
    c) Salt Lake City, Utah

890. In the 1800s the Northeast and West of the United States became closer as a result of the _____.
    a) **railroad**
    b) **steamboat**
    c) **airplane**

891. When Ronald Reagan became president for the first time, people said, "The United States has gone from peanuts to popcorn." Which former president owned a big peanut farm? _____.
    a) **Gerald Ford**
    b) **George Washington Carver**
    c) **Jimmy Carter**

892. Most **U.S. presidents** have been trained as _____.
    a) lawyers
    b) educators
    c) entertainers

893. Eleven states share a border with Canada. Two of them are _____.
    a) **California** and **Illinois**
    b) **Maine** and **Washington**
    c) **Connecticut** and **Maryland**

894. The **Peace Corps** began in the _____.
    a) 1960s
    b) 1890s
    c) 1980s

895. **Florida** and **Alaska** are both _____.
    a) peninsulas
    b) islands
    c) gulfs

896. **In the 1800s** families traveled West by _____.
    a) car
    b) wagon
    c) ship

897. **Plantations** were large farms in the _____.
    a) West
    b) South
    c) Northeast

898. Iowa and Nebraska are located in the _____.
    a) **Coffee Belt**
    b) **Banana Belt**
    c) **Corn Belt**

899. Who said, "Talk softly and carry a big stick?" _____.
   a) **Henry Kissinger**
   b) **Lyndon Johnson**
   c) **Theodore Roosevelt**

900. **Ralph Nader** is a lawyer who helps _____.
   a) consumers
   b) children
   c) women

901. **Eire**, **Ontario**, **Oklahoma**, **Alabama** and **Connecticut** are _____.
   a) French names
   b) Indian names
   c) German names

902. "**We Shall Overcome**" was a popular song _____.
   a) during the Civil War
   b) during the Revolutionary War
   c) during the freedom marches of the 1960s

903. **Old Hickory** was the nickname of the seventh president. His real name was _____.
   a) Stonewall Jackson
   b) Andrew Jackson
   c) Michael Jackson

904. From 1609 to 1664 New York City was ruled by the_____.
   a) **Spanish**
   b) **English**
   c) **Dutch**

905. In 1775 **Paul Revere** rode his horse at midnight to warn _____.
   a) the British about the Colonists
   b) the Colonists about the British
   c) the Indians about the French

906. Who landed in North America almost 1000 years ago? _____.
   a) **Lief Ericson**
   b) **Henry Hudson**
   c) **Marco Polo**

907. **Aspen** and **Vail** are best known for _____.
   a) skiing
   b) sailing
   c) surfing

908. In 1677 **William Penn** was the first person to write a charter separating _____.
   a) business and government
   b) church and state
   c) national and state government

909. The **U.S. Supreme Court** members are approved by the Senate after being _____.
    a) elected by the people
    b) selected by the Senate
    c) appointed by the president

910. People at the **Pentagon** talk about _____.
    a) education
    b) defense
    c) health

911. **Yellowstone**, **Zion**, **Yosemite**, **Acadia** and **Shenandoah** are the names of _____.
    a) National Parks
    b) Indian cities
    c) religious organizations

912. **Three Southern states** are _____.
    a) South Dakota, Iowa and Nevada
    b) Georgia, Mississippi and South Carolina
    c) Missouri, California and Arizona

913. The **largest city in the West** is _____.
    a) Los Angeles
    b) Seattle
    c) Denver

914. The continental United States is divided into _____.
    a) **two time zones**
    b) **three time zones**
    c) **four time zones**

915. When the United States bought **Alaska**, it cost _____.
    a) two cents an acre
    b) two dollars an acre
    c) two hundred dollars an acre

916. **Abraham Lincoln** _____.
    a) died of old age
    b) was killed soon after the Civil War
    c) died of pneumonia

917. When **Ronald Reagan** became president for the second time, he was _____.
    a) 53 years old
    b) 63 years old
    c) 73 years old

918. **The Equal Rights Amendment** (ERA) is designed to help _____.
    a) women
    b) minorities
    c) immigrants

Grammar

PART TWO

Directions: Complete the sentences.

919. Joe is hurrying because he must _____.
    a) to leave immediately
    b) leaves immediately
    c) leave immediately

920. I know Jennifer doesn't like her job, but most _____.
    a) people is happy to have a job
    b) people are happy to have a job
    c) peoples are happy to have a job

921. Steven will go to the party if he _____.
    a) will have time
    b) does have time
    c) has time

922. I need _____.
    a) two million and a half dollars
    b) two and a half million dollars
    c) two and a half millions dollars

923. I wonder where _____.
    a) he lives
    b) does he live
    c) lives he

924. I hope it will not be too _____.
    a) trouble for you
    b) many troubles for you
    c) much trouble for you

925. Where can I get _____?
    a) information about your country
    b) informations about your country
    c) an information about your country

926. When you are sick, you should avoid _____.
    a) smokes
    b) smoking
    c) to smoke

avoid
enjoy 932

927. We had a wonderful time _____.
    a) spend a few hours together
    b) to spend a few hours together
    c) spending a few hours together

928. Classes _____.
    a) are from nine to three
    b) are at nine to three
    c) begin from nine to three

929. Mrs. Lewis' doctor advised her to move to _____.
    a) another state
    b) the other state
    c) other state

930. Derek is tired _____.
    a) so he went to sleep late last night
    b) because he went to sleep late last night
    c) but he went to sleep late last night

931. If I had a car, _____.
    a) I'll drive to school
    b) I'd drive to school
    c) I drove to school

932. When Dahlia has free time, she enjoys _____.
   a) swim
   b) to swim
   c) swimming

933. A dollar is the _____.
   a) same as four quarters
   b) many as four quarters
   c) much as four quarters

934. Nurses are people who _____.
   a) takes care of sick people
   b) are taking care of sick people
   c) take care of sick people

935. It snowed _____.
   a) very hard to go outside
   b) so hard to go outside
   c) too hard to go outside

936. Why don't we _____?
   a) has pizza tonight
   b) going to have pizza tonight
   c) have pizza tonight

937. It's too cold _____.
   a) to swim
   b) for swim
   c) that we can't swim

938. Billie Jean King plays tennis often because _____.
   a) she very enjoys it
   b) she enjoys it a lot
   c) a lot she enjoys it

939. John wishes he _____.
   a) has more free time
   b) will have more free time
   c) had more free time

940. If Mr. and Mrs. Moffat didn't live in Alaska, they _____.
   a) would visit their relatives in California more often
   b) visited their relatives in California more often
   c) should visit their relatives in California more often

941. He was so tired _____.
   a) that he fell asleep on the bus
   b) as he fell asleep on the bus
   c) then he fell asleep on the bus

942. The Empire State Building is one of the _____.
    a) tallest building in the world
    b) tallest buildings in the world
    c) most tall buildings in the world

943. Anyone who wants to learn a language _____.
    a) should speak to native speakers
    b) shall speak to native speakers
    c) spoke to native speakers

944. When Georges was a child, he _____.
    a) can't play ball
    b) couldn't play ball
    c) couldn't to play ball

945. Last winter Gloria was walking on ice when she _____.
    a) was slipping and breaking her hand
    b) slipped and broke her hand
    c) has slipped and broken her hand

946. Many people in the United States think _____.
    a) the milk is good for the children
    b) the milk is good for children
    c) milk is good for children

947. When you want to know the time, you ask "Do you have _____?"
    a) the time
    b) a time
    c) time

948. After his second heart attack, John stopped _____.
    a) to smoke
    b) smoking
    c) smoke

949. One of my friends _____.
    a) are from Korea
    b) come from Korea
    c) is from Korea

950. Who _____?
    a) washed the dishes
    b) did wash the dishes
    c) did washed the dishes

951. If you were the teacher, _____?
    a) will you give homework
    b) did you give homework
    c) would you give homework

952. Tell me what time _____.
    a) you get home
    b) do you get home
    c) will you get home

Directions: Answer the questions.

953. When did Prince Charles marry Princess Diana?
    a) He married with her in 1981.
    b) He married her in 1981.
    c) He got married with her in 1981.

954. Is it going to rain?
    a) I think.
    b) I think it.
    c) I think so.

955. Are the Satos going to visit their son?
    a) It is depend on the situation.
    b) It depends on the situation.
    c) It depends the situation.

956. When are you going to study for your exam?
    a) I'd like to study tonight.
    b) I like to study tonight.
    c) I will like to study tonight.

957. What did he say?
    a) He said me he was busy.
    b) He told me he was busy.
    c) He told to me he was busy.

958. When was Andrea born?
    a) She born in 1977.
    b) She is born in 1977.
    c) She was born in 1977.

959. Does Mr. Scarlatti understand the instructions?
    a) No, he has still confused.
    b) No, he is still confused.
    c) No, he still confused.

960. Which one of your sons plays basketball?
    a) Dani does. He's the tallest of the three.
    b) Dani does. He's the taller of the three.
    c) Dani does. He's the most tall of the three.

961. Why were there so many mistakes?
    a) She typed too quickly.
    b) She typed so quick.
    c) She typed too quick.

962. Why can't anyone answer the telephone?
    a) Everyone are busy.
    b) Everyone is busy.
    c) Everyone seem busy.

963. What did your teacher do?
    a) He explained me the answer.
    b) He explained the answer to me.
    c) He to me explained the answer.

964. When do you think you'll be home?
    a) As soon as I can.
    b) As soon that I can.
    c) So soon as I can.

965. Who won the race?
    a) A seven-year-old girl.
    b) A seven-years-old girl.
    c) A seven-years-olds girl.

966. When will she return?
    a) Next summer, after she will finish dental school.
    b) Next summer, after she is going to finish dental school.
    c) Next summer, after she finishes dental school.

967. How did you get here?
    a) I had to take a taxi because I was late.
    b) I have to take a taxi because I was late.
    c) I must take a taxi because I was late.

968. Who wrote *A Farewell to Arms*?
    a) It was wrote by Ernest Hemingway.
    b) It was writing by Ernest Hemingway.
    c) It was written by Ernest Hemingway.

969. Do I have to give up rich desserts?
    a) Yes, you absolutely may.
    b) Yes, you absolutely must.
    c) Yes, you absolutely might.

Directions: Read the first sentence in each item. Then choose the correct second sentence.

970. What he said sounds too good to be true.
    a) Do you believe him?
    b) Are you believing him?
    c) Are you believe him?

971. Teresa is only two years old.
    a) She isn't enough old to go to school.
    b) She isn't old enough to go to school.
    c) She isn't very old to go to school.

972. When Moses Malone was ten, he was over five feet tall.
    a) He was tall his age.
    b) He was tall at his age.
    c) He was tall for his age.

973. I think that woman was on TV last night.
    a) Do you know what is her name?
    b) Do you know what name she has?
    c) Do you know what her name is?

974. Evan is a computer specialist.
    a) He worked here since July.
    b) He has worked here since July.
    c) He works here since July.

975. Harris always knows what's happening in the world.
    a) That's because always he reads the newspaper.
    b) That's because he reads the newspaper always.
    c) That's because he always reads the newspaper.

976. That television show isn't interesting at all.
    a) It's bored.
    b) It's boring.
    c) It bores.

977. Joe said, "Don't forget to lock the door."
    a) I said, "I don't."
    b) I said, "I'm not."
    c) I said, "I won't."

978. What a lazy man!
    a) He don't do nothing.
    b) He doesn't do nothing.
    c) He doesn't do anything.

979. When the truck hit Mrs. Perdue, she was knocked down and badly hurt.
    a) A few minutes later, she rushed to the hospital.
    b) A few minutes later, she was rushed to the hospital.
    c) A few minutes later, she is rushing to the hospital.

980. Don says it's difficult to learn two foreign languages at the same time.
    a) I am agree.
    b) I am agreeing.
    c) I agree.

981. He has only two short sleeve shirts.
    a) One is blue; the other is gray.
    b) One is blue; other is gray.
    c) One is blue; another is gray.

982. You must be thirsty.
    a) Are you wanting some lemonade?
    b) Do you want some lemonade?
    c) Are you want some lemonade?

983. Henry is tired.
    a) He'd rather eat at home.
    b) He'd rather to eat at home.
    c) He'd rather eats at home.

984. The chemicals can explode.
    a) You don't have to smoke near them.
    b) You mustn't smoke near them.
    c) You couldn't smoke near them.

985. New guests must check in.
    a) All other guests go directly to the dining room.
    b) All other guest go directly to the dining room.
    c) All other go directly to the dining room.

986. Your ring is beautiful.
    a) Show it me again.
    b) Show it to me again.
    c) Show me it again.

987. Dr. Stram is busy now.
    a) She'll speak to you later.
    b) She speaks to you later.
    c) She has spoken to you later.

988. How long have they been gone?
    a) I haven't seen them for two weeks.
    b) I haven't seen them since two weeks.
    c) I haven't seen them during two weeks.

989. I'm not working at this time.
    a) I wish I were working.
    b) I wish I am working.
    c) I wish I worked.

990. Who's watching the baby?
    a) The boy what lives next door.
    b) The boy where lives next door.
    c) The boy who lives next door.

991. The bus is late.
    a) We've been waiting for fifty minutes.
    b) We've been waiting on fifty minutes.
    c) We've been waiting with fifty minutes.

992. Our electric bill is high.
   a) Please remember to turn off the lights before you leave.
   b) Please remember turn off the lights before you leave.
   c) Please remember turning off the lights before you leave.

993. I'm new in this neighborhood.
   a) Do you know a place where I can get good meat?
   b) Do you know a place somewhere I can get good meat?
   c) Do you know a place anywhere I can get good meat?

994. My car uses a lot of gas.
   a) I wish it won't use so much.
   b) I wish it doesn't use so much.
   c) I wish it didn't use so much.

995. Carl has two jobs.
   a) He has fewer free time than his wife does.
   b) He has less free time than his wife does.
   c) He has little free time than his wife does.

Directions: Find a sentence that means the same as the one given.

996. There is no rule that says you must pay in advance.
   a) You don't have to pay in advance, but you can.
   b) You shouldn't pay in advance, but you can.
   c) You mustn't pay in advance, but you can.

997. Natalie studied in Mexico from 1982 to 1984.
   a) She has been studying there for two years.
   b) She studied there for two years.
   c) She has studied there for two years.

998. Ramon came to the United States five years ago. He's still living in the United States today.
   a) He lived in the United States for five years.
   b) He lives in the United States for five years.
   c) He has been living in the United States for five years.

999. There is a fifty percent chance of rain tomorrow.
   a) It might rain tomorrow.
   b) It will rain tomorrow.
   c) It shall rain tomorrow.

1000. You can't take this course if you don't pay.
   a) You should pay before you take this course.
   b) You have to pay before you take this course.
   c) You may pay before you take this course.

1001. Sam was rich but now he's poor.
   a) He is used to being poor.
   b) He used to be poor.
   c) He used to be rich.

Guide to Illustrations

General Knowledge about the United States *Part One*
Top row (left to right): Albert Einstein (#15); MD (#26); Elvis Presley (#21)
Bottom row: VIP (#8)

Phrases and Idioms *Part One*
Top row (left to right): cock-a-doodle-do (#163)
Middle row: to make a toast (#649)
Bottom row: a lemon (#156); a broken heart (#132)

American Holidays and Special Occasions *Part One*
Top row (left to right): cap and gown (#182); holly (#705); New Year's Eve (#194)
Bottom row: wedding day (#236); Thanksgiving Day (#173); Flag Day (#211)

Vocabulary *Part One*
Top row (left to right): H_2O (#290); hammer (#294)
Middle row: umbrella (#315); skyscraper (#264)
Bottom Row: quack, quack (#322)

American History, Geography and Government *Part One*
Top row (left to right): American flag (#365); George Washington (#356); NASA (#411); Sally Ride (#378)
Bottom Row: The Big Apple (#341); The Empire state (#407)

Grammar *Part One*
Top row (left to right): half past eight (#443)
Second row: There's going to be an important meeting (#495)
Third row: Which is more expensive (#460)
Bottom row: I didn't see you at the office yesterday (#498)

General Knowledge about the United States *Part Two*
Top row (left to right): one dollar bill (#508)
Middle row: March comes in like a lion (#521); baby shower (#505)
Bottom row: Marx Brothers (#547)

Phrases and Idioms *Part Two*
Top row (left to right): dead end street (#588)
Bottom row: hold your horses (#655); on the nose (#650); baseball (#590, 611, 636); two left feet (#626)

American Holidays and Special Occasions *Part Two*
Top row (left to right): Easter rabbit (#677); Martin Luther King (#671)

Bottom row: flags (#674); Christmas tree (#716, 719); groundhog (#704, 728); Season's Greetings (#675)

Vocabulary   *Part Two*
Top row (left to right): highchair (#753); conductor (#774); magician (#792)
Bottom row: bald (#818); an island (#825)

American History, Geography and Government   *Part Two*
Top row: John Hancock (#876)
Bottom row: Republican Party (#850); Statue of Liberty (#849); John F. Kennedy (#981); Abraham Lincoln (#872, 916)

Grammar   *Part Two*
Top row (left to right): will have/does have/has (#921)
Middle row: take/takes/are taking (#934)
Bottom row: should speak/shall speak/spoke (#943)

Answer Key

General Knowledge about the United States   *Part One*

1. b	15. b	29. b	43. a	57. b	71. b
2. a	16. c	30. a	44. c	58. a	72. c
3. a	17. b	31. c	45. c	59. b	73. c
4. b	18. b	32. c	46. c	60. c	74. a
5. c	19. c	33. a	47. c	61. b	75. b
6. b	20. a	34. b	48. b	62. c	76. a
7. c	21. c	35. a	49. a	63. b	77. c
8. a	22. b	36. b	50. b	64. a	78. c
9. c	23. c	37. c	51. c	65. c	79. a
10. a	24. c	38. a	52. b	66. b	80. b
11. a	25. c	39. c	53. a	67. a	81. c
12. a	26. b	40. b	54. a	68. c	82. a
13. c	27. a	41. a	55. c	69. c	83. b
14. b	28. c	42. b	56. c	70. a	84. b

Phrases and Idioms   *Part One*

85. b	99. b	113. a	127. b	141. b	155. c
86. c	100. a	114. c	128. a	142. a	156. b
87. a	101. c	115. b	129. b	143. b	157. b
88. b	102. c	116. a	130. a	144. a	158. c
89. a	103. a	117. b	131. a	145. a	159. c
90. a	104. b	118. a	132. c	146. c	160. a
91. c	105. a	119. c	133. a	147. a	161. a
92. c	106. a	120. a	134. b	148. b	162. b
93. c	107. c	121. c	135. b	149. c	163. c
94. b	108. b	122. a	136. b	150. a	164. b
95. b	109. b	123. b	137. c	151. b	165. c
96. a	110. a	124. a	138. b	152. a	166. a
97. c	111. a	125. c	139. a	153. b	167. c
98. b	112. c	126. c	140. c	154. b	

American Holidays and Special Occasions   *Part One*

168. a	182. b	196. c	210. b	224. b	238. c
169. b	183. c	197. a	211. c	225. c	239. a
170. c	184. c	198. b	212. c	226. b	240. a
171. a	185. a	199. b	213. b	227. c	241. a
172. c	186. b	200. b	214. b	228. c	242. b
173. c	187. a	201. c	215. c	229. b	243. a
174. a	188. b	202. b	216. a	230. c	244. c
175. b	189. c	203. a	217. a	231. a	245. b
176. a	190. c	204. b	218. c	232. b	246. c
177. a	191. b	205. c	219. a	233. c	247. a
178. b	192. c	206. c	220. b	234. c	248. a
179. a	193. a	207. a	221. c	235. b	249. c
180. b	194. b	208. c	222. c	236. c	250. c
181. c	195. c	209. a	223. b	237. c	

Vocabulary   Part One

251. c	265. a	279. b	293. c	307. b	321. c
252. b	266. b	280. a	294. a	308. b	322. c
253. c	267. c	281. c	295. a	309. a	323. a
254. a	268. b	282. a	296. b	310. a	324. b
255. b	269. a	283. c	297. b	311. c	325. a
256. a	270. b	284. b	298. a	312. a	326. c
257. b	271. c	285. a	299. a	313. c	327. b
258. b	272. a	286. c	300. b	314. b	328. a
259. a	273. a	287. c	301. c	315. c	329. b
260. a	274. a	288. b	302. b	316. c	330. b
261. c	275. c	289. b	303. a	317. a	331. b
262. c	276. a	290. a	304. b	318. c	332. c
263. b	277. c	291. c	305. b	319. c	333. a
264. c	278. b	292. b	306. c	320. b	

American History, Geography and Government   Part One

334. b	348. a	362. a	376. c	390. b	404. a
335. a	349. c	363. c	377. a	391. a	405. a
336. c	350. c	364. b	378. b	392. c	406. c
337. a	351. a	365. c	379. b	393. c	407. a
338. b	352. a	366. b	380. a	394. b	408. c
339. b	353. a	367. a	381. a	395. c	409. b
340. c	354. c	368. a	382. b	396. c	410. b
341. a	355. b	369. c	383. c	397. b	411. a
342. b	356. a	370. b	384. a	398. b	412. c
343. b	357. c	371. c	385. c	399. b	413. a
344. c	358. b	372. b	386. b	400. b	414. c
345. a	359. a	373. c	387. c	401. c	415. b
346. b	360. c	374. a	388. a	402. a	416. c
347. b	361. a	375. b	389. b	403. b	417. c

Grammar   Part One

418. c	432. c	446. c	460. c	474. c	488. b
419. a	433. a	447. c	461. c	475. a	489. b
420. a	434. a	448. a	462. b	476. b	490. c
421. c	435. a	449. a	463. c	477. b	491. c
422. b	436. b	450. b	464. a	478. a	492. b
423. a	437. c	451. b	465. c	479. b	493. a
424. a	438. b	452. c	466. b	480. c	494. c
425. b	439. a	453. a	467. a	481. b	495. a
426. a	440. c	454. a	468. c	482. b	496. b
427. b	441. b	455. b	469. b	483. c	497. a
428. a	442. b	456. c	470. c	484. b	498. b
429. b	443. b	457. b	471. c	485. b	499. a
430. c	444. a	458. b	472. a	486. c	500. c
431. b	445. b	459. a	473. b	487. a	

General Knowledge about the United States   Part Two

501. a	505. a	509. c	513. c	517. b	521. a
502. b	506. b	510. c	514. a	518. b	522. a
503. c	507. c	511. c	515. a	519. c	523. c
504. c	508. a	512. b	516. a	520. c	524. b

525. a	535. b	545. c	555. b	565. c	575. b
526. a	536. b	546. b	556. a	566. b	576. b
527. c	537. c	547. b	557. b	567. a	577. a
528. a	538. a	548. c	558. b	568. c	578. b
529. c	539. b	549. c	559. c	569. c	579. c
530. a	540. b	550. b	560. b	570. a	580. a
531. b	541. a	551. a	561. a	571. b	581. c
532. c	542. c	552. a	562. b	572. a	582. b
533. c	543. a	553. b	563. c	573. c	583. a
534. c	544. a	554. a	564. a	574. a	584. a

Phrases and Idioms   *Part Two*

585. a	599. a	613. c	627. c	641. a	655. a
586. b	600. c	614. a	628. c	642. c	656. a
587. a	601. c	615. c	629. b	643. b	657. c
588. c	602. a	616. a	630. a	644. a	658. b
589. a	603. b	617. c	631. a	645. c	659. c
590. c	604. c	618. a	632. a	646. b	660. b
591. b	605. b	619. b	633. b	647. b	661. b
592. c	606. a	620. a	634. a	648. c	662. c
593. c	607. b	621. b	635. c	649. c	663. b
594. a	608. c	622. c	636. b	650. a	664. b
595. c	609. c	623. c	637. a	651. a	665. a
596. b	610. b	624. b	638. c	652. a	666. a
597. a	611. c	625. b	639. a	653. b	667. a
598. b	612. b	626. a	640. c	654. a	668. c

American Holidays and Special Occasions   *Part Two*

669. c	683. c	697. a	711. c	725. b	739. b
670. c	684. b	698. c	712. b	726. a	740. a
671. b	685. a	699. c	713. a	727. b	741. b
672. b	686. b	700. a	714. c	728. b	742. c
673. a	687. a	701. c	715. c	729. c	743. c
674. b	688. c	702. a	716. b	730. c	744. a
675. a	689. b	703. c	717. c	731. b	745. b
676. a	690. c	704. b	718. b	732. c	746. a
677. b	691. b	705. a	719. a	733. a	747. b
678. c	692. a	706. b	720. c	734. b	748. b
679. c	693. a	707. c	721. c	735. b	749. a
680. c	694. b	708. b	722. a	736. b	750. c
681. a	695. b	709. c	723. b	737. b	751. b
682. b	696. a	710. a	724. c	738. b	752. c

Vocabulary   *Part Two*

753. c	762. c	771. c	780. c	789. a	798. b
754. b	763. b	772. b	781. a	790. a	799. a
755. b	764. b	773. a	782. c	791. c	800. b
756. c	765. b	774. c	783. b	792. c	801. a
757. c	766. c	775. b	784. a	793. b	802. c
758. a	767. a	776. a	785. b	794. a	803. b
759. c	768. a	777. c	786. c	795. c	804. a
760. a	769. b	778. b	787. c	796. b	805. a
761. a	770. c	779. a	788. a	797. c	806. c

807. c	812. b	817. b	822. a	827. c	832. c
808. b	813. c	818. c	823. c	828. a	833. c
809. b	814. b	819. c	824. a	829. b	834. b
810. a	815. a	820. c	825. b	830. a	835. a
811. b	816. a	821. b	826. c	831. a	

History, Geography and Government   *Part Two*

836. c	850. c	864. a	878. b	892. a	906. a
837. c	851. c	865. b	879. a	893. b	907. a
838. a	852. c	866. a	880. c	894. a	908. b
839. b	853. a	867. b	881. b	895. a	909. c
840. c	854. b	868. c	882. c	896. b	910. b
841. b	855. c	869. a	883. b	897. b	911. a
842. a	856. a	870. b	884. a	898. c	912. b
843. a	857. b	871. b	885. c	899. c	913. a
844. b	858. c	872. a	886. a	900. a	914. c
845. b	859. b	873. c	887. b	901. b	915. a
846. a	860. c	874. a	888. b	902. c	916. b
847. c	861. a	875. c	889. a	903. b	917. c
848. b	862. b	876. b	890. a	904. c	918. a
849. c	863. c	877. c	891. c	905. b	

Grammar   *Part Two*

919. c	933. a	947. a	961. a	975. c	989. a
920. b	934. c	948. b	962. b	976. b	990. c
921. c	935. c	949. c	963. b	977. c	991. a
922. b	936. c	950. a	964. a	978. c	992. a
923. a	937. a	951. c	965. a	979. b	993. a
924. c	938. b	952. a	966. c	980. c	994. c
925. a	939. c	953. b	967. a	981. a	995. b
926. b	940. a	954. c	968. c	982. b	996. a
927. c	941. a	955. b	969. b	983. a	997. b
928. a	942. b	956. a	970. a	984. b	998. c
929. a	943. a	957. b	971. b	985. a	999. a
930. b	944. b	958. c	972. c	986. b	1000. b
931. b	945. b	959. b	973. c	987. a	1001. c
932. c	946. c	960. a	974. b	988. a	

General Knowledge about the United States
PART ONE

General Knowledge about the United States
PART TWO

Phrases and Idioms
PART ONE

Phrases and Idioms
PART TWO

American Holidays and Special Occasions
PART ONE

American Holidays and Special Occasions
PART TWO

American History, Geography and Government
PART ONE

American History, Geography and Government
PART TWO

Vocabulary
PART ONE

Vocabulary
PART TWO

Grammar
PART ONE

Grammar
PART TWO

FREE CHOICE	*General Knowledge about the United States*	*Phrases and Idioms*	*American Holidays and Special Occasions*	**FREE CHOICE**

FREE CHOICE				**FREE CHOICE**
General Knowledge about the United States **and** *Grammar*				*American Holidays and Special Occasions* **or** *Vocabulary*
Phrases and Idioms **or** *American History, Geography and Government*				**Opponents Choice**
Opponents Choice				*Vocabulary* **and** *American History, Geography and Government*
American Holidays and Special Occasions **or** *Phrases and Idioms*				*General Knowledge about the United States* **or** *Grammar*

FREE CHOICE	*Grammar*	*American History, Geography and Government*	*Vocabulary*	**FREE CHOICE**

117